A TASTE OF PRISON
Custodial conditions for trial and remand prisoners

ROY D.KING
Department of Sociology and Social Administration
University of Southampton

and

RODNEY MORGAN
School of Humanities and Social Sciences
University of Bath

ROUTLEDGE DIRECT EDITIONS

ROUTLEDGE & KEGAN PAUL
London, Henley and Boston

First published in 1976
by Routledge & Kegan Paul Ltd
39 Store Street,
London WC1E 7DD,
Broadway House,
Newtown Road,
Henley-on-Thames,
Oxon RG9 1EN and
9 Park Street,
Boston, Mass. 02108, USA
Manuscript typed by Alice Rockwell
Printed and bound in Great Britain
by Unwin Brothers Limited,
The Gresham Press, Old Woking, Surrey
A member of the Staples Printing Group
© Roy D.King and Rodney Morgan 1976

ISBN 0 7100 8407 2

A TASTE OF PRISON

Routledge Direct Editions

CONTENTS

PREFACE

In 1952, Sir Lionel Fox, then Chairman of the Prison Commission, wrote that the conditions for the unconvicted in local prisons 'have never excited public comment of a general nature'. Times have changed and we hope that this short monograph will play a part in a public debate that could lead to a real change in those conditions - which could only be for the better.

Fox looked forward to the establishment not only of remand centres to take unconvicted and unsentenced young persons out of the local prisons where they were then housed, but also to the setting up of observation and classification centres which would perform the remand function, and much else besides, for adults. In the familiar British experience of cut backs and compromise, the observation and classification centres were never built. And while the philosophy of individualised treatment which lay behind the planning of the centres has now largely been consigned to Prison Department archives in favour of a more realistic, even hard-faced, approach to the problems of confining the criminal, the legacy of that era remains - in the nomenclature, location and use of training prisons and the distribution of resources within the prison system. Most, though far from all, young offenders are now housed in remand centres before trial or sentence. But, as we argue in this monograph, the remand centres have largely duplicated the regime and conditions in the impoverished, overcrowded local prisons which continue to house their adult counterparts. The local prisons remain, as in Fox's day, the Cinderellas of the prison service - bearing the brunt of its burden but losing out drastically in terms of capital expenditure. In an age when security has come to dominate the handling of sentenced prisoners, there is good reason to reconsider the situation of persons detained in custody before trial or sentence - persons who, though they may never be sentenced to imprisonment, get their taste of it just the same.

Fox was inclined to think that the conditions for untried and unsentenced prisoners which he described were 'perhaps the best that can be provided in the local prisons as they are' though he thought it would be reasonable, in a newly designed prison, to provide for them a 'separate block with its own work-room in which the rooms were of a higher standard than ordinary cells and more comfortably

furnished'. Even such a minimal specification would doubtless be
welcomed by anyone who has been held in custody on remand. But
there is no sign of its being achieved. And much more than that is
needed if we are to maintain a civilised standard of containment
compatible with the enlightened ideology of an advanced industrial
democratic society. In our view such a standard can only be achieved if there is a willingness to re-examine the role of the local
prisons in the prison system and to re-invest in them: and if we
are prepared to rewrite the Rules governing the custody of unconvicted and unsentenced prisoners.

The findings reported in this monograph form part of an on-going
programme of research which began in 1968 when one of us (RDK) was
awarded a grant by the Home Office Research Unit to investigate the
nature of prison regimes. In part the object of the 'Prison Regimes
Project' was to develop measures of regimes which could be used to
make systematic comparisons between the experiences of different
groups of prisoners in different prisons. In the course of the project pilot work was conducted at a number of Prison Department establishments and fieldwork was carried out at HM Prisons Albany,
Ford, Camp Hill, Coldingley and Winchester and at HM Remand Centre
Winchester. In the present volume we focus on those parts of our
data which relate to the unconvicted and unsentenced prisoners at
the local prison and remand centre at Winchester. A further volume
on the development and changes in the regime at Albany prison is in
preparation and publication of the comparative aspects of the study
is planned.

It can never be easy to do research in prisons. Research workers
who are unable to demonstrate their independence from the authorities are unlikely to command much respect either from prisoners or
from the academic community. On the other hand, research workers
who are insensitive to the realities of prison administration are
unlikely to receive much co-operation from members of a service
which seldom gets a good press. We have not thought it appropriate
in the present volume to spend much time discussing the methodology
of the research, or to describe the relationships between the research team and the staff and prisoners, or to give any treatment of
the problems and rewards of doing research in prison for researchers
and respondents. These matters will be dealt with in depth in
future publications. It is all the more important, therefore, that
we record our gratitude to all those involved in the prison service,
either as keepers or kept, who have contributed so generously of
their time - which was not always their own - and energies to enable
this work to be done. Rarely can a programme of research have been
conducted in prisons with such wholehearted co-operation both from
the staff at Prison Department and from the staff and prisoners in
each of the establishments in which we spent so much time. That we
repay them with such forthright criticism is testament, we believe,
both to their appreciation of the value of research and to our concern with the problems which they face and share. We gave an undertaking to all our respondents that we would be willing to discuss
any comments as to the facts in our drafts from interested parties -
the staff at Head Office, the executive of the Prison Officers' Association and, in some cases and in so far as it remained relevant
for them, representatives of the staff and prisoners in the prisons

themselves. Our undertaking was to listen and to discuss. If we
could not be convinced that we were wrong, we would simply have to
agree to disagree. While we recognise that some of our criticisms
may be wounding - what University Department would welcome research
workers into their midst for months at a time? - we believe that we
have not said anything that we cannot justify from the repeated
observations which we carried out. That we have not held anything
back goes without saying - and the absence of certain criticisms
that have been made with some force in the USA and elsewhere should
provide some comfort both for the prison service and for the
community.

.It remains for us to thank the many others to whom we owe debts
in respect of the present volume. We have said that the research
was supported by a grant from the Home Office Research Unit and we
should like to thank Stella Cunliffe, the former director, and John
Croft, the present director, for allowing us to persuade them that
it was worth extending the project from training prisons into the
local prison at Winchester. We are grateful to Ken Dawson and
Stanley Clarke at the Prison Department for their help in setting up
the facilities, and to Tom Hayes, former Director of the South West
Region, for smoothing our path into the prison. Both the Research
Unit and Prison Department have offered comments, on points of fact
and method. None of their comments affected the substance of our
findings or argument, and we have been happy to benefit from their
remarks. To the governor, staff and prisoners at Winchester and
Winchester Remand Centre our debt is obvious but should not go un-
recorded. We made many friends there. The Prison Officers' Association lent their support to the study which we gladly accepted.
Since the Association has not offered comments on the draft we
assume that they do not fundamentally disagree with what we have
said in this report.

The research was carried out from the Department of Sociology and
Social Administration at the University of Southampton. It would
not have got off the ground and still less have been completed without the enduring support and encouragement of John Smith and John
Martin. Since the completion of the fieldwork Rodney Morgan moved
to the University of Bath where the continued support of Stephen
Cotgrove facilitated some of the writing-up for this monograph. Roy
King would particularly like to thank the Ford Foundation for the
award of a fellowship which enabled him to spend 1973 in the Department of Sociology at Yale. During that time he was able, among
other things, to discuss this work with Al Reiss, and Stan Wheeler
as well as Dan Freed from the Law School and gained greatly from
doing so. He was also able to prepare a preliminary draft.

We owe more than we can adequately say to Kenneth Elliott and
Robin Williams who worked with us throughout the project. Any merit
which this project may have is a result of their work at least as
much as our own. That they have not shared in the writing, as they
did in the design and the fieldwork, is because they moved to the
Universities of Leeds and Durham respectively. We think that they
broadly share our views, though the responsibility for the contents
of this report must inevitably rest with us. Aubrey McKennell and
Andrew Bebbington of the University of Southampton have at various
times advised on, and carried out, statistical analysis. Without

their expert guidance on scaling we would not have been able to make the kinds of regime comparisons which we had set ourselves to do. Several persons have given us clerical and secretarial assistance in the course of the project, but Christina Cluett bore the brunt of typing with a cheerfulness which our handwriting did not always deserve. Our final thanks are due to those very busy people who still took so much trouble to read, and comment on, various stages of the draft: Ken Elliott, John Martin, Dan Freed and Michael Zander. Had we heeded all their helpful criticisms we would have written a different book: where possible we have taken their advice but where we have not done so we hope they will understand why.

We completed our manuscript in 1974. Since then there have been a number of developments, which do not lead us to change our conclusions, but without reference to which our study would obviously be incomplete. We discuss them briefly in a postscript.

RDK, Southampton

RM, Bath

January 1976

Chapter 1

THE REMAND FUNCTION IN A CHANGING PRISON SYSTEM

From a legal standpoint the establishments maintained by the Prison Department in England and Wales receive four main groups of persons from the courts. First, there are those who have been convicted of criminal offences and sentenced to periods of custody in prisons, borstals or detention centres, with or without the option of a fine. In 1972 (at the time of writing the most recent year for which figures were available: see Cmnd 5489, 1973) the 55,783 male and 1,947 female receptions in this category accounted for 44.3 per cent of the male and 31.4 per cent of the female admissions to these institutions. Second, there are persons who have not been convicted in the courts but who, for a variety of possible reasons, are deemed to require safe custody before or during trial. Within this category came 42,261 male and 2,240 female receptions or 33.6 and 37.9 per cent respectively of the 1972 totals. Third, there are persons who have been convicted of criminal offences but who have not yet been sentenced. These persons may be detained because they have been committed by the magistrates to a higher court for sentence or because the magistrates, or higher courts, are unable or unwilling to decide immediately on disposal. Usually, though not always, this is because the courts require medical or social enquiries to be carried out before passing sentence. The 22,212 male and 1,673 female receptions of convicted but unsentenced prisoners comprised 17.6 and 28.1 per cent respectively of the total receptions in 1972. Lastly there are civil prisoners. This group includes persons who have been detained in custody as a means of coercion or as a punishment for failing to obey court orders generally in respect of debts, as well as some aliens and illegal Commonwealth immigrants awaiting deportation. The remaining 4.5 per cent of male and 1.3 per cent of female receptions in 1972 were accounted for by 5,657 and 82 cases respectively in this category.

This monograph will be mainly concerned with unconvicted prisoners and to a lesser extent with unsentenced prisoners. Of course the same person may be received into prison several times in the same year under the same or different legal circumstances. The fact that some people are remanded in custody before or during trial, and then for reports after conviction, before finally receiving a sentence of imprisonment means that the number of receptions is

always to some degree greater than the number of persons actually
involved (Fox, 1952, p.111; HORU, 1960, p.37). In 1972, for example, 42.3 per cent of the 22,212 male prisoners received after
conviction and awaiting sentence, had previously been remanded in
custody before trial in conjunction with the same offence. But what
is of central concern is that large numbers of persons are received
into prison, before either trial or sentence, and are not subsequently sentenced to penal custody by the courts.

In 1972 45.6 per cent of all males and 73.2 per cent of all
females remanded in custody, as either unconvicted or unsentenced
prisoners or both, subsequently received non-custodial sentences.
A further 3.7 per cent of the males, and 4.2 per cent of the females
were found not guilty. The fact that in 1972 25,100 male and 2,494
female persons (the over-riding majority of all unsentenced women
prisoners) spent varying periods of time in prisons and remand
centres but were subsequently dealt with in the community, and that
a further 2,044 males and 142 females were found not guilty after a
period in custody, raises several questions for research and policy.

Most research studies to date, in Britain at least, have been
concerned with the judicial aspects of the use of custody before
trial or sentence, especially the circumstances under which magistrates decide to remand on bail or in custody, and the relationship
between such decisions and subsequent disposal. Most recently these
matters have been the subject of a working party into 'Bail Procedures in Magistrates' Courts' (Home Office, 1974). There has been
some dispute as to whether or not the fact that almost half the
persons held in custody before trial or sentence subsequently receive non-custodial sentences, indicates that this use of custody is
unjustified. The use of custody on remand has declined in recent
years. Of all persons coming before magistrates' courts 20.4 per
cent were remanded in custody in 1972 compared with 33.9 per cent in
1967. If the actual number of persons remanded in custody has
fallen rather less dramatically this is a reflection of the greatly
increased number of cases with which the courts have had to deal.
It may, of course, be argued that the decision to refuse bail does,
and should, involve criteria other than those which lead to a custodial sentence following conviction. Evidence of the likelihood of
the defendant failing to attend his trial, or of committing other
offences prior to trial, or of interfering in some way with the
course of justice if granted bail, is not necessarily a sufficient
indication of the need for a custodial sentence (Home Office, 1974).
Furthermore it may be argued that the period of the remand in custody is taken into account at the sentencing stage so that either
longer sentences of imprisonment, or any form of custody, is thereby
avoided (HORU, 1960). And finally it must be noted that not all of
those persons who are received into prison prior to trial or
sentence remain so until the time of sentence: part-bail is not revealed by prison statistics and is an aspect of court practice which
requires evaluation if assertions concerning the unnecessary use of
custody are adequately to be assessed.

On the other side of the debate it must be said that if decisions
to refuse bail are based on criteria substantially different from
those which lead to custodial sentences then there is a disturbingly
high likelihood that persons who become unconvicted or unsentenced

prisoners will subsequently become sentenced prisoners (Bottomley, 1970 and 1974; Davies, 1971; HORU, 1960; HORU, 1974; M.King, 1971). It is not possible to gauge the degree to which the fact of pre-sentence custody itself influences the sentence of the court. What is clear is that in making bail decisions, the courts, and the police upon whose recommendations the courts appear largely to depend (Bottomley, 1970 and 1974; HORU, 1974; Zander, 1971) place greatest weight on the seriousness of the offence and the previous record of the accused. This information is often used not only as prima facie evidence of the likelihood of the accused absconding or committing further offences, or obstructing justice, but also at a subsequent stage of the need for a custodial sentence.

In recent years it has been suggested that the courts might make greater use of their powers for employing alternatives to custody for obtaining reports and for ensuring that the accused is brought to trial without hindrance to the judicial process (Davies, 1971; Zander, 1967, 1971; M.King, 1971). Section 53 of the Criminal Justice Act 1972 enabled probation and after-care committees with financial assistance from the Home Office, to establish bail hostels and this provision may aid the courts to use alternatives.. But at the time of writing only one bail hostel exists in the whole country and its twelve beds in London are currently under-occupied (Advisory Council, 1974, para.457; 'Guardian', 5 March 1973; Blom-Cooper, 1973). And although the recent working party on bail procedures recommends both the extension of hostel provision and a presumption in favour of unconvicted persons being granted bail, the authors of the report are not convinced that the present evidence suggests excessive use of custody nor do they recommend that any such presumption should be granted in favour of convicted persons (Home Office, 1974).

The question of whether the use of custody for unconvicted or unsentenced persons is 'justified', however, is by its very nature incapable of resolution simply by reference to the evidence. In each case a judgment has to be made, and just what judgment is made will depend on whether one adopts a 'law and order' perspective or a 'civil rights' perspective. This is not to say that the accumulation of evidence will be unimportant in influencing the climate of opinion within which bail or custody decisions are made. The legal debate concerning such decisions will rightly continue as more evidence becomes available: and in chapter five we are able to add to that body of evidence with our analysis of the 'remand careers' of persons passing through the remand centre at Winchester during the first three months of 1971. But it is to say that whatever the evidence there is little likelihood that the use the courts make of the remand in custody before trial, or the committal for enquiry before sentence, will diminish in the foreseeable future.

It seems important therefore that we acknowledge, however reluctantly, that large numbers of persons will continue to be held in custody and that a substantial proportion of those persons will, either before or at sentence, be released to the community. This fact has implications in addition to those which have so far preoccupied researchers into the legal aspects of the process. The social consequences of detention other than under the sentence of the court, the conditions under which such detention is served, and the demands this makes on the resources of a prison system geared to the custody of sentenced prisoners, require thorough and urgent examination - from the point of view of the community on whose behalf that system is said to function no less than the individuals who pass through it. At least one British study has included within its brief the wider consequences of bail refusal for the families of accused persons in terms of loss of work, income or accommodation (M.King, 1971). One other study has provided some documentation of the daily routine for prisoners awaiting trial at Risley Remand Centre (Davies, 1970). But while both prison administrators and academic penologists have pointed to the burden that the remand and trial function places on the prison system (see for example, Fox, 1952; Sparks, 1971) all too little material has been published that would permit a systematic analysis of the extent of that burden. None the less the problem of dealing with unconvicted and unsentenced prisoners cannot sensibly be discussed except in the context of the organisation and working of the prison system as a whole.

As has often been noted, if seldom adequately reflected upon, the widespread use of custody as a punishment is of comparatively recent origin. By contrast the use of custody prior to sentence has a long history. The common gaols established by Henry II in the twelfth century existed primarily for the safe custody of persons awaiting trial; and the judges who went on circuit were concerned not to fill the gaols but to empty them. But by the time of Edward I the gaols had begun to assume a coercive function especially in relation to persons who could not, or would not, meet their debts or fines; and they retained this function over the centuries despite the growth of specialist establishments for debtors and others in contempt of court, such as the infamous King's Bench, Marshalsea and Fleet prisons, and from the seventeenth century, the Houses of Correction. The gaols and Houses of Correction were not amalgamated to form the local prisons until 1865 although by this date these institutions had become virtually indistinguishable in their penal function whatever the intentions behind the original Bridewell.

Although the courts have had power since mediaeval times to pass sentences of imprisonment as a punishment for certain offences this facility was little exercised and was outweighed by the use of fines, banishment, ordeals, execution and an exotic array of corporal punishments. Not until the late eighteenth and early nineteenth century did imprisonment become, with the exception of the death penalty, the most serious sanction which could be imposed by a court. It is undoubtedly the case that by this time a troubled industrial society was looking to the concept of institutional confinement to solve a multitude of problems (Foucault, 1967; Rothman, 1971). Even so it is doubtful whether the use of penal servitude and imprisonment at hard labour in the convict prisons would have then developed had it not been for pressure to find an alternative to the then current form of banishment - transportation initially to North America and subsequently to Australasia. When the administration of both local and convict prisons passed to the central control of the newly-formed Prison Commission in 1878 the basis of the modern prison system was formed. It was from the reform of the convict prisons that the obsessive twentieth century concern with applying custodial treatment for convicted prisoners has emerged.

Excluding the borstals and detention centres the prison system today consists of approximately eighty establishments. Over half of these are institutions the titles of which have changed over the years rather more frequently than their functions, but which are now known as 'training' prisons. Today training prisons range in security from the open prisons which receive mainly Category D prisoners under the Mountbatten classification (Cmnd 3175, 1966, para.217) to the so-called 'dispersal' prisons advocated by the Radzinowicz Report (Advisory Council, 1968, para.32) which cater for the longer sentence, high security risk Category A and Category B prisoners. Between these extremes come closed medium security institutions largely housing prisoners in Category C who are thought not to have the 'stability to be kept in conditions where there is no barrier to their escape' (Cmnd 3175, 1966, para.217). The remainder are the local prisons, twenty-three for men and one for women, and the ten remand centres, three of which accommodate both men and women. Most of the remand centres house persons under 21 years. Only one takes adult males, while the three which receive women, because they draw small numbers from huge catchment areas, take adults as well as girls.

The local prisons, and to a lesser extent the remand centres, have inherited virtually all of the functions of the common gaols and Houses of Correction, and to these several new ones have been added. The first responsibility of these local establishments is to the courts. They receive persons before and during trial and are charged with their safe custody and with escorting them to and from the higher courts. Increasingly they are required to hold prisoners for enquiry before sentence and to furnish the facilities whereby such enquiries may be carried out. They also continue to receive all civil prisoners. In addition they receive all prisoners sentenced to imprisonment or borstal, and are required to undertake the categorisation and allocation of these offenders to training prisons, young prisoner centres and borstal institutions. The training prisons and borstals on the other hand only receive their prisoners on transfer from the local prisons and remand centres. In fact, in spite of the expressed ideal of the Home Office that all convicted prisoners should be sent to training prisons with a regime suited to their needs (Cmnd 4214, 1969, para.171), about half of all the sentenced prisoners received into local prisons are never transferred to training prisons but serve the whole of their sentences in those same local prisons (Sparks, 1971). Finally the local prisons may serve a number of functions in relation to prisoners who have already been transferred to training prisons. All local prisons, and those remand centres housing women, provide a temporary location for some long sentence prisoners to enable them more easily to receive accumulated visits from their families. Some local prisons provide hospital or other specialist facilities for prisoners transferred to them for treatment, and some provide hostel facilities for the pre-release employment scheme to which long-term prisoners may be transferred shortly before the end of their sentences, and from which they may go out to work in the community. And both local prisons and remand centres may receive prisoners on transfer from training prisons or borstals for production at court in respect of further charges.

In 1959 the White Paper 'Penal Practice in a Changing Society' diagnosed the essential problem of local prisons as follows: they 'have to perform too many specialist functions for which they are not adequately equipped. Built as they were 100 years or more ago ... they are in themselves quite unfitted to modern conceptions of penal treatment' and 'they stand as a monumental denial of the principles to which we are committed' (Cmnd 645, 1959, paras 54-7). According to the White Paper the remedy for this situation would involve the building of sufficient specialised institutions to re- lieve the local prisons of their trial and remand and allocation functions. Moreover new open training prisons, providing a greater range of facilities, would further skim off the population in the local prisons which would then be in a position to do what they 'ought to be doing' - providing 'an effective training programme for prisoners with shorter sentences' (para.62) who had been sent there not 'because there is nowhere else to send (them)' but 'because that is the right place for (them)' (para.64).

Sir Lionel Fox, the then Chairman of the Prison Commission, is generally acknowledged to have been the driving force behind the White Paper. It is said that he had been greatly influenced by the recommendations of the 1951 United Nations World Health Organisation seminar on the medical, psychological and social examination of of- fenders which stressed the need for observation, diagnosis and classification as a basis for sentencing, treatment and research (Klare, 1964). Certainly the proposals for creating a number of 'observation and classification' centres which were to be built adjacent to, and share staff with, the remand centres reflected the correctional optimism and reformist principles to which the members of that seminar subscribed. The White Paper acknowledged that no remand centres - which had been authorised under the Criminal Justice Act of 1948 - had yet been built because of financial re- strictions and other difficulties although preliminary work on the first was to begin that very year. The observation and classifi- cation centres were to perform the same functions for adults that remand centres were supposed to fulfil for younger offenders. That is to say, the new centres would deal not only with the custody of untried prisoners, and the preparation of court reports on the un- sentenced, but also with the classification of those already sentenced to imprisonment and their allocation to appropriate places for training.

The proposals for observation and classification centres have never come to fruition although as recently as 1965, Hall Williams could refer optimistically to the likely effects of the 'extensive network' of nine remand centres for persons under 21 and the four centres at Risley, Thorp Arch, Low Newton and Pucklechurch, which were then planned for adults by the Prison Department. In fact, by the end of that year, all but one of the remand centres now in use were already in existence. By 1970 the nine remand centres for boys, two of which also cater for women and girls had been com- pleted, but only Risley, which also accommodates females and boys, had materialised for adult males (Cmnd 4724, 1971, App.3). Risley was opened in 1965 and the following year the planned extension of Low Newton for adult males was all that remained in the building programme for adults - and the accommodation for this had been cut

from 200 to 120 (Cmnd 3408, 1967, App.2). Two years later the proposal for dealing with adults at Low Newton had been dropped altogether (Cmnd 4186, 1969, App.2) and no further remand centres for
adult males have either been built or planned. In the Prison Department report for 1972 it was said that three new remand centres
were nearing completion, three existing centres were in the process
of being, or were to be, extended, and planning permission and sites
were being sought for a further two, one of which, in the Midlands,
was to house women and girls only (Cmnd 5375, 1973, App.2). However
at the time of writing plans for the Midlands centre had apparently
been dropped ('Hansard' vol.855, cols 1441-5, May 1973). None of
these developments or plans is designed to cater for adult males.

A decade after the publication of 'Penal Practice in a Changing
Society' the attempt to change the multifunctional nature of the
local prison had been abandoned - although the policy of extending
the range of training prisons was to be pursued with even greater
vigour. A new White Paper 'People in Prison' announced that remand
centres were to be left 'to deal with those under 21' (Cmnd 4214,
1969, para.148). The local prisons, under Government plans involving 'a major, though gradual, shift of policy' were to retain their
traditional trial-and-remand function for adult male prisoners as
well as providing for the allocation and categorisation of convicted
prisoners, medical examination and treatment, and pre-release
arrangements for long sentence prisoners (para.165). It is not entirely clear what is meant by 'a major, though gradual, shift of
policy' because, apart from Risley, the policy set out by 'Penal
Practice' had never been carried into effect, and the functions outlined in 'People in Prison' were already being carried out in some
local prisons. Since this latest White Paper did not refer directly
to the custody of sentenced prisoners in local prisons, except
during allocation and categorisation, it had to be presumed that the
essential shift in policy was to be the transfer of more convicted
offenders, who were not suitable for open conditions but who were
unlikely to be escape risks, from the local prisons to the proposed
new Category C prisons (para.172). Such a presumption was confirmed
by the more explicit declaration of policy in the Annual Report of
Prison Department for 1971 (Cmnd 5037, 1972, para.26).

In 1969 the Prison Department envisaged the building of six Category C prisons each of which might hold up to 800 prisoners serving
sentences up to eighteen months as well as a number of more secure
establishments for longer sentence prisoners. But it was clear that
a building programme on this scale would not eliminate the function
of providing custody for the convicted prisoner who spends the
whole, or a substantial part, of his sentence in the local prison.
Those serving 'very short sentences' (Cmnd 4214, 1969, para.170)
would presumably not be transferred to the training prisons, and as
for the rest, the new prisons were expected to 'relieve the
pressure' (para.172) on the local prisons rather than to empty them.
This kind of relief was, of course, part of the policy put forward
by Fox in 'Penal Practice in a Changing Society' except that in
those days of optimism - before the Mountbatten and Radzinowicz
Reports - it was hoped that the increase in accommodation would come
in the form of open prisons (Cmnd 645, 1959, para.94). By 1971 a
considerable increase in the number of prison places for which

planning clearance was held was announced (Cmnd 5037, 1971, para.30)
and the long term aim was stated to be the accommodation of all
prisoners serving six months or more in training prisons (para.26).
Even so the 'major, but gradual, shift of policy' may have meant
only that the local prisons would stay as they were because, at
least until 1971, the new building programme could have done no more
than catch up with the dramatic increase in the prison population.
Since 1971 the picture has changed somewhat. In 1973 and 1974 the
Prison Department reported falls in the daily average population and
it remains to be seen whether the further substantial building
programme of Category C accommodation announced in 1973 (Cmnd 5375,
App.2) will be maintained in view of this decline.

Over the years, however, one can hardly fail to detect a more
profound change in penal thought and policy, the long term implications of which are not as yet clear. It is true that there has
been little departure from the description given in 'Penal Practice
in a Changing Society' of the multi-functional local prisons.
Nevertheless the decision not to build adult observation and classification centres was significant. The air of optimism underlying
the 1959 White Paper is almost totally absent from its successor.
Fox placed his faith in observation, diagnosis and classification
and believed that research would play a major part in facilitating
these processes. Though such themes were still present in 1969 they
were introduced in a much lower key. In 'People in Prison' the
emphasis shifted to the harsh realities: the need to provide
'humane containment' (para.15) in 'secure' establishments (para.16),
the inconclusive results of much prison research (paras 120-1), and
the frank admission that 'neither our capacity for the diagnosis of
the needs of offenders nor the ability to effect a cure is at
present as great as many advocates of this or that form of treatment
have implied' (para.32). This more pessimistic tone regarding the
constructive possibilities of custody finds its most forceful and
recent expression in this country in the 1974 Report of the Advisory
Council on the Penal System, 'Young Adult Offenders'. The Council
takes the view that although custody may be justified by considerations of public protection or general deterrence, or even as a
stop-gap whilst community resources are being investigated, 'neither
practical experience nor the results of research in recent years
have established the superiority of custodial over non-custodial
methods in their effect upon renewed offending' and that 'comparisons of different types of custodial regimes have so far shown
little or no difference in effects upon offending again' (para.157).
The conclusion to which the Advisory Council comes on the basis of
this assessment is very clear. 'While a simple form of classification is obviously required before a decision is made, for instance
between open and closed conditions, the choice of different kinds of
custodial regimes is not as varied as to justify prolonged assessment of the personal characteristics of most offenders.' In any
case, the Council argues, 'any custodial establishment with an adequate induction system and reasonable flexibility in its facilities
should be capable of receiving satisfactorily all offenders sent to
it and of picking out for transfer the small minority who require
specialist attention which cannot be provided within it'(para.51).

The Advisory Council was concerned with young offenders, persons

who whether at present detained in borstals, detention centres or
prisons are, for the most part, spending nine months or less in
custody. Clearly the adult sentenced population does include a significant number of long term prisoners whose detention in the kind
of all-purpose 'neighbourhood' institutions proposed by the Advisory
Council for young persons (paras 319-20) would be considered un-
satisfactory. Nevertheless it must be conceded that if any of the
Advisory Council's conclusions and recommendations are found con-
vincing in relation to young offenders then they must in many respects be accepted for adults also. But if that were the case then
the specialised nature of training prisons envisaged in 'Penal
Practice' and re-emphasised in 'People in Prison' would seem much
less important or desirable and the need for elaborate observation,
diagnosis, classification and so on would virtually disappear. We
may be thankful that the unrealistic belief in the efficacy of a
policy of observation, diagnosis and classification advocated by Fox
has been given the lie. But we will certainly regret that the
building programmes of recent years – the most extensive and expensive in our history – have concentrated on the development of so
many more or less secure, and more or less isolated 'training'
prisons instead of the observation and classification centres and
remand centres which, had they been built in the right places, could
have been converted for use in a framework of re-developed local or
neighbourhood prisons. In 1972 over 80 per cent of all sentenced
prisoner receptions were for sentences of eighteen months or less.
Among the average daily population for that year more than 40 per
cent had sentences of eighteen months or less and over 80 per cent
sentences of less than four years. Had the building programme been
different the majority of these prisoners might well have been
housed in decent conditions in neighbourhood prisons, with specialist institutions catering only for those persons who were screened
out on grounds of mental disturbance, and those long sentence
prisoners whose notoriety, disruptive behaviour or escape potential
seemed to require specially secure regimes.
   Were the Prison Department to accept these views, and there can
be no doubt that the climate of opinion as reflected in 'People in
Prison' indicates that this possibility is much more likely than was
the case in 1959, then there will clearly be a need to reappraise
the functions of the local prison, including its trial and remand
function. We return to these matters in our final chapter following
our discussion of present resources and their utilisation.

Chapter 2

TRIAL AND REMAND PRISONERS IN THE PRISON POPULATION

If the local prison is to continue as a multiple-function institution, it is important to know just what functions are being performed, for whom, and in what conditions.

The local prisons have long been overcrowded. 'Overcrowding' in
the prison system is determined not by reference to desirable
standards of accommodation or facilities, nor even by reference to
areas of square feet per person or staff-prisoner ratios: it is
measured by the numbers of persons presently living and sleeping in
cells which were designed for the most part a century or more ago
for one person. Not since before the Second World War have all
prisoners been accommodated one to a cell (Cmnd 2030, 1962, p.12).
In 1959 it was acknowledged that even if all the untried prisoners
were removed from the local prisons, together with the 2,000 persons
serving three years or more whom it was then hoped to transfer
elsewhere, there would still be 1,500 men sleeping three in a cell;
a degree of overcrowding rightly said to be intolerable (Cmnd 645,
1959, para.86).

In 1964 the Prison Department overcame their distaste for allowing two prisoners to share a cell, but by the end of the following
year only 350 men were so housed while more than 5,000 were accommodated three to a cell. The average number of prisoners sharing
cells jumped by more than 3,000 in 1966, fell slightly in 1967 and
1968, only to soar to record heights since then. In 1970 there
were on average over 13,500 prisoners sharing cells and the fall in
numbers during the following three years has been only marginal.

Although the Prison Department announced the spreading of overcrowding to selected training prisons in 1970, when for a time one
in four prisoners in these establishments were said to be sharing
cells (Cmnd 4724, 1971, para.27), an examination of the statistics
on accommodation and population given in the Appendices of the
Annual Reports of the Prison Department shows that some listed
training prisons, such as Chelmsford, Lancaster, Nottingham and
Stafford, have been persistently overcrowded in recent years. In
the years 1971 and 1972 the only closed training prison for women,
and nine out of the thirty-one for men, were overcrowded. But
whilst there is evidence that the burden is being spread a little,
the brunt of overcrowding has traditionally been borne by the local

prisons, and that is still the case. In 1971, as for many years past, every local prison held many more prisoners on average than its officially stated capacity. In 1972 two local prisons, Swansea and Wandsworth held numbers marginally below their total capacity while the other twenty-two, including Holloway, were still over-crowded. Several of these prisons held on average one-and-a-half times their stated capacity and on occasion in 1972 two local prisons, Leeds and Canterbury, came close to holding twice the number for whom they officially had places.

Overcrowding does exist elsewhere in Prison Department establish-ments. In recent years borstals would undoubtedly have been over-occupied were it not for the fact that through its control of the period spent in custody, the Prison Department is able to limit the numbers held at any one time. But it is in the new remand centres and especially at Ashford and Risley that the conditions which have long beset the local prisons have been most closely duplicated. Table 2.1 shows the extent of overcrowding in remand centres and the different types of prisons for males and females over the last few years by comparing the average daily population with the officially rated cellular or dormitory capacity for each type of institution.

During the years 1967-72 the average daily population in local and open training prisons fluctuated somewhat although both types of institution ended the period much as they had begun. It is more difficult to compare the certified accommodation in these insti-tutions because of a change in recording procedures introduced in 1971. In that year Prison Department included so-called 'special' accommodation in hostels and hospitals for the first time on the ground that places were not maintained elsewhere in the system for persons so housed. Since the places in hostels and hospitals had long been a feature of the system it seems evident that Prison De-partment was merely reflecting a change of use that had been forced upon it by the rise in population whereby beds elsewhere could no longer be maintained for these persons. Thus the special accommo-dation represents an increase that is more apparent than real. If this accommodation is excluded it is clear that both the local prisons and the open prisons underwent a marginal decline in the accommodation available over the period. As a result the local prisons remained dramatically over-used with over two-fifths more prisoners on average than certified places. The open prisons, by contrast, remained relatively under-used. It is true that the use of open prisons has been more effective in the last few years com-pared to 1968 when, under the joint pressures of the Mountbatten Report (Cmnd 3175, 1966) and the introduction of the parole scheme, the use of open prisons fell to a low of 72.9 per cent of capacity. But this has been achieved as much by reducing accommodation and putting establishments such as Eastchurch to other uses as by in-creasing transfers from local prisons. It must also be said that the under-use indicated by these figures is almost certainly mis-leading. Much open prison accommodation is of the dormitory type in camp huts taken over from the armed forces. Anyone who has seen the absurdly cramped conditions in some of these dormitories will be aware of the ambiguities involved in defining overcrowding by refer-ence to 'certified accommodation' rather than some more objective standard.

TABLE 2.1 Certified accommodation and average daily population in prisons and remand centres for males and females 1967-72

	Local prisons			Remand centres			Open training prisons			Closed training prisons		
	Accomm	ADP	% use	Accomm	ADP	% use	Accomm	ADP	% use	Accomm	ADP	% use
1967	10948	15213	139	1336	1470	110	4470	3964	89	7321	6995	96
1968	10619	13293	125	1338	1442	108	4447	3238	73	7664	7343	96
1969	10374	14800	143	1356	1748	129	4309	3392	79	8295	7617	92
1970	10476	16766	160	1443	2094	145	4126	3739	91	8911	8655	97
1971	10773	16403	152	1509	2029	134	4336	3957	91	9422	9712	103
1972	10654	15299	144	1569	2115	135	4359	3742	86	9957	10067	101
% change 1967-72	97	101	104	117	144	123	98	94	97	136	144	105

Source: Appendix 3 on accommodation and population from Annual Reports of the Prison Department, 1967-72. Note that in 1971 Prison Department changed the basis for calculating accommodation in prisons by including 'special' accommodation in hostels and hospitals. Accommodation of this kind provided 886 places in 1971 and 1,071 in 1972 for local prisons; 263 and 262 places in remand centres; 48 and 48 in open prisons; and 251 and 257 in closed prisons. Since the inclusion of special accommodation would have the effect of artificially increasing the apparent number of places we have excluded it from this table to maintain the comparison with earlier years for which the figures are not available.

The pattern for the closed training prisons and the remand centres over the period has been very different. They experienced a more or less steadily increasing average population, with numbers in 1972 some 44 per cent up in both cases over the 1967 figures. Both also benefited from an increase in certified accommodation, though when the special hostel and hospital accommodation is once again eliminated, this was much greater for the closed training prisons than the remand centres. The increase by more than a third in accommodation in the closed training prisons was achieved largely by the opening of new establishments and the recommissioning or genuine expansion of old ones. Northeye, Coldingley, Eastchurch, Portsmouth, Reading, Long Lartin, Northallerton, Ranby, Swinfen Hall and Acklington have all been opened or reopened since 1967. It is apparent that the closed training prisons at least until 1970 were as full as is compatible with the logic of the system as outlined in 'People in Prison', bearing in mind the need for some spare capacity to permit reasonable transfer and allocation: and that in 1971-2 they became somewhat too full. In 1972, Camp Hill, Lancaster, Nottingham, Preston, Shepton Mallet and Stafford prisons were suffering degrees of overcrowding comparable to the most sorely pressed local prisons.

The equivalent increase in the remand centre population, however, has been absorbed without the benefit of a large scale building programme. There were in 1972 nine remand centres. Eight of these had been opened by 1965 and the ninth, Latchmere House, formerly a senior detention centre, was brought into commission in November 1970 to provide an extra 130 places. No new blocks at existing centres were opened, and indeed the remand centre at Holloway, which in 1969 provided 40 places for girls, was closed in 1970. If the artificial increase accounted for by the recording of 262 places in 'special' accommodation is ignored there was a modest improvement by some 233 places in 1972 over 1967. Since, as far as we have been able to discover, no new building was involved it seems likely that even this was achieved largely by a revised definition of what constitutes overcrowding - that is by a more intensive use of cells through doubling up and by taking over rooms originally designed for other purposes. Certainly this seems to have been the case at Winchester Remand Centre which we discuss in chapter four. Even so, in 1972, the overcrowding in remand centres generally was very nearly as bad as that in the much more widely publicised local prisons.

The most striking fact to emerge from Table 2.1 then, is that in spite of the increase in accommodation in closed training prisons and the more intensive use of those facilities there has been no dramatic reduction in the overcrowding in local prisons. And Prison Department has been markedly reluctant to improve matters by taking up the slack in open prisons. Indeed the recent announcement of the closure of two open prisons ('The Times', 1 August 1974) indicates that this option is finally being relinquished. Although the downturn in population since 1970 has eased the situation somewhat the local prisons were none the less more overcrowded in 1972 than they had been five years earlier. Of course it is difficult to predict the future and things may yet change for the better. Estimates of the prison population, however, have been notoriously unreliable.

Just as the estimates in 'People in Prison' were considerably below the actual rate of increase for 1969-70, so the estimates contained in the White Paper 'Public Expenditure to 1975-76' (Cmnd 4829, 1971, p.45) were grossly exaggerated. But as successive prison population estimates since 1971 have been reduced so too has the building programme. In 1973, 9,700 places were planned over five years (Cmnd 5519, 1973) instead of the 14,000 places which had been envisaged in the previous year for a similar period (Cmnd 5178, 1972). If the latest figures come anywhere near the mark, and if the current building programme is not further curtailed, then the numbers of persons sleeping two or three to a cell will certainly be reduced. But if the experience of the recent past is anything to go by there seems little likelihood that we will soon return to the pre-war standard of one man one cell: at least so long as it is left to Prison Department to try to match the building programme to the estimated population, and for so long as that building programme concentrates on closed training prisons instead of the local prisons themselves.

For whom do our overcrowded local prisons and remand centres have to cater? Almost all of the persons over the age of 21 years, and a small proportion of those under 21, are received initially into the local prisons for varying periods of time. Most, though by no means all, of those under 21 and a few of those over 21 are received into the remand centres. But while a great deal of work is generated by the processes of reception and discharge it is the actual population over a period of time, rather than the receptions during that period, for whom the local prisons and remand centres have to provide on-going facilities. While data on the characteristics of persons received into prison have been available for some years, official information on the characteristics of the prison population is sparse. The work of Banks (1968) at Parkhurst and Blundeston and Sparks (1971) at Winson Green has compensated for the official lack of figures to some degree, at least so far as the sentenced population is concerned.

The relationship between the numbers and characteristics of the annual receptions into the local prisons and remand centres and the size and constitution of the average daily population in different types of Prison Department establishments is a complex one. For sentenced prisoners account has to be taken not only of the length of sentences imposed by the courts but also of departmental policies regarding transfers within the prison system, and of the success of prisoners in keeping their remission or gaining parole, and, in the case of fine defaulters, of paying their way out of prison. Similarly for the unconvicted, unsentenced and civil receptions such matters as length of time awaiting trial, the time it takes to furnish reports, the speed with which deportation is effected and the possibility of paying debts or otherwise complying with court orders will all affect the population statistics. Obviously receptions of persons on remand for comparatively short periods will have a much smaller influence on the cumulative population than receptions under sentence, some of which are for very long periods indeed. But a review of the official figures over the last decade or so shows that both the receptions and the population of unconvicted and unsentenced prisoners of all ages are growing proportion-

TABLE 2.2 Receptions and population in Prison Department establishments for males and females of all ages 1960–72

		Receptions			Increase 1960=100		Population			Increase 1960=100	
		1960	1968	1972	1968	1972	1960	1968	1972	1968	1972
Untried prisoners	M	26,229	38,274	44,891	146	171	1,388	1,836	2,923	132	211
	F	1,496	2,229	2,827	149	189	44	99	133	225	302
	Total	27,725	40,503	47,718	146	172	1,432	1,935	3,056	135	213
Unsentenced prisoners	M	9,869	17,905	19,582	181	198	590	1,145	1,560	194	264
	F	1,281	1,222	1,086	95	85	63	75	81	119	129
	Total	11,150	19,127	20,668	172	185	653	1,220	1,641	187	251
Civil prisoners	M	8,059	6,984	5,657	87	70	382	472	493	124	129
	F	271	164	82	61	30	11	5	4	45	36
	Total	8,330	7,148	5,739	86	69	393	477	497	121	126
Sentenced prisoners	M	40,514	47,650	55,783	118	138	23,838	28,203	32,372	119	136
	F	2,481	1,608	1,947	65	78	783	626	762	80	97
	Total	42,995	49,258	57,730	115	134	24,621	28,829	33,134	117	135

Note: Figures for receptions and population are given in several places in the Annual Reports and Statistical Tables published by the Prison Department. Often slightly different figures are given for a particular category, though usually the totals agree. On occasions the figures given in different places are widely discrepant. Moreover the figures given in the reports for earlier years are sometimes corrected in the reports for later years. We have used the corrected statistics given in the Summary of Reception and Population Figures to be found on page 2 of the Annual Statistical Tables. However to achieve consistency, we have always included 'aliens not under sentence' together with 'civil prisoners' as has been done in the latest reports (and not with 'untried prisoners' as was the case in earlier years), and persons remanded under Section 26 of the Magistrates' Courts Act 1952 under 'untried prisoners' (and not 'convicted prisoners awaiting sentence or enquiry' as became the case in 1972).

ately faster than the receptions and population of sentenced persons. Table 2.2 gives the changes in annual receptions and average population since 1960 for the main classes of prisoners in all Prison Department establishments. 1968 and 1972 are the most appropriate years to take for consideration of current prison population trends. Between 1960 and 1968 there was a steady though modest increase in the daily average population. There then followed a period of extravagant increase and not until 1972 had the population levelled out and fallen to a point in keeping with the upward trend observable during the 1960s. The same trend is broadly reflected in the overall reception statistics. From 1954 to 1967 prison receptions rose steadily. In 1968, largely as a result of measures introduced by the 1967 Criminal Justice Act, receptions fell substantially. But the Act, and in particular the introduction of suspended sentences, produced a backlog and by 1970 receptions were at a record level for recent years (they were much higher at the beginning of this century) only to decline again in 1971 and 1972. So whilst the rate of increase for both population and receptions has been persistently upwards it has not been constant nor has it applied to all categories of prisoners or equally to males and females.

In 1960 untried and unsentenced prisoners together accounted for 43.1 per cent of all receptions and 7.7 per cent of the total population in prisons, borstals and detention centres. By 1972 these groups accounted for 51.8 per cent of receptions and 12.3 per cent of the population. Put another way, more than two-thirds of the increase in receptions and more than a fifth of the increase in population for all categories of prisoners between 1960 and 1972 is attributable to the rise in numbers of persons imprisoned before trial or sentence.

The reception of civil prisoners has fluctuated widely since 1960 although the general trend has been downwards, and in the case of female civil prisoners dramatically downwards. This fall in numbers, plus the rise in receptions in other categories, means that civil prisoners formed only 4.4 per cent of total receptions in 1972 compared to 9.2 per cent in 1960. The proportion of civil prisoners in the population, however, has remained roughly constant throughout the decade at about 1.5 per cent suggesting that there has been some increase in the length of time that civil prisoners spend in prison. The considerable decline in the number of female civil prisoners both received and held is hardly reflected in the total figures for this category because of the very small number of women involved.

In contrast to the one-and-three-quarters to two-and-a-half-fold increase in the receptions and population of untried and unsentenced prisoners, the numbers of sentenced prisoners received have risen by only 34 per cent and their numbers in the population by the same amount. Of course the numbers of sentenced prisoners were already large in 1960 and so even this more modest increase added by far the largest group of more than 8,500 persons to the average daily population. But whereas sentenced prisoners had formed 47.7 per cent of all receptions in 1960 and 90.9 per cent of the total population these proportions had fallen to 43.8 per cent and 86.5 per cent respectively by 1972. Again it should be noted that these figures very largely represent the position regarding male sentenced prisoners. The number of sentenced females received and held fell during the 1960s and has only recently begun to increase again, but because of the relatively small numbers involved this contrasting trend has had only a marginal influence upon the aggregate figures for both sexes.

These figures, given for prisoners of all ages, mask certain important differences within each of the categories which need to be taken into account when assessing the tasks of the local prisons and remand centres. Among sentenced prisoners the largest increase was for those sentenced to borstal training or custody in detention centres where the receptions increased by 321 per cent over the period and the population by 159 per cent. This meant that growing pressure was felt on establishments for young offenders: indeed so much so that for a time in 1970 the Prison Department could only meet the demand for borstal places by progressively reducing the period of custodial training, and by increasing the waiting period that many had to spend in local prisons and remand centres before allocation (Cmnd 4724, 1971, para.29). The situation in the borstals had eased somewhat by 1971 so that waiting periods were reduced (Cmnd 5037, 1972, paras 112-15). Similar patterns emerge in other prisoner categories. The increases in receptions and population both of untried and unsentenced prisoners have been somewhat greater for persons under the age of 21 than for those over 21 years. Since remand centres have very largely taken over the custody of this younger age group from the local prisons this trend deserves greater scrutiny.

Remand centres are 'places for the detention of persons not less than fourteen but under twenty-one years of age who are remanded or committed in custody for trial or sentence' (Criminal Justice Act 1948, s.48). As we have seen the concept of adult observation and classification centres introduced by the White Paper 'Penal Practice in a Changing Society' (Cmnd 645, 1959) has been abandoned leaving a single remand centre, Risley, receiving adult males and females as well as persons under 21 years and Low Newton and Pucklechurch receiving women and girls, to remind us of the venture. Whilst remand centres may take persons aged 14 to 17 years they do not normally do so. Section 23 of the Children and Young Persons Act 1969 provides that a person under the age of 17 years who is remanded or committed for trial and who is not given bail shall be committed to the care of the local authority unless a court certifies that he is so unruly that he cannot safely be committed to such care. In these circumstances, a person aged 14 and under 17 years must then be committed to a prison or remand centre. Any young person who is committed to the Crown Court with a view to a borstal sentence, under Section 28 of the Magistrates' Courts Act 1952 must similarly be sent to a prison or remand centre. The Secretary of State also has the power to direct, under Section 53 of the Children and Young Persons Act 1933, that a young person found guilty of certain serious offences should be located in a remand centre. The extent to which remand centres constitute an alternative to local authority provision is important because there has been a disproportionate increase not only in the numbers of persons under 21 but also under 17 years of age being received into institutions managed by Prison Department.

From Table 2.3 it can be seen that the rate of increase for re-

TABLE 2.3 Receptions and population of untried and unsentenced prisoners in Prison Department establishments by sex and age 1960-72

		Receptions			Increase on 1960 = 100		Population			Increase on 1960 = 100	
		1960	1968	1972	1968	1972	1960	1968	1972	1968	1972
Untried prisoners under 21	M	7,039	12,011	14,952	171	212	403	567	914	141	227
	F	482	976	1,114	202	231	11	44	46	400	418
	Total	7,521	12,987	16,066	173	214	414	611	960	148	232
Untried prisoners over 21	M	19,190	26,263	29,939	137	156	985	1,269	2,009	129	204
	F	1,014	1,253	1,713	124	169	33	55	87	167	264
	Total	20,204	27,516	31,652	136	157	1,018	1,324	2,096	130	206
Unsentenced prisoners under 21	M	4,434	8,502	10,077	192	227	259	514	790	198	305
	F	599	638	560	107	93	27	43	35	159	130
	Total	5,033	9,140	10,637	182	211	286	557	825	195	288
Unsentenced prisoners over 21	M	5,435	9,403	9,505	173	175	331	631	770	191	233
	F	682	584	526	86	77	36	32	46	89	128
	Total	6,117	9,987	10,031	163	164	367	663	816	181	222

Note: For sources see note to Table 2.2.

ceptions and average daily population of untried and unsentenced prisoners of both sexes has been consistently greater for persons under 21 years of age than it has for adults. In the single category where numbers have fallen, the reception of female unsentenced prisoners, the decrease has been very much less for persons under 21 years than for those over 21 years. In 1960 32 per cent of the receptions and 34 per cent of the population of untried and unsentenced prisoners were under 21 years: by 1972 these proportions had risen to 39 per cent and 38 per cent. Put another way, of the increase of 29,511 receptions in these categories between 1960 and 1972 almost half, 14,149 receptions, are accounted for by persons under 21 years.

This evidence of population pressure in the age group which remand centres were designed to serve does much to explain the overcrowding to which the centres were early subject. Those who framed the 1948 Criminal Justice Act hoped, among other things, to extend the range of disposal alternatives available to the courts, especially when sentencing young persons, and every effort was to be made to ensure that young persons should not experience prison prior to sentence. Indeed in the case of sentences to a detention centre the court was required first to ascertain that a place was available so that following sentence the person could go direct from the court to the centre and not, as was and is the case with borstal trainees, be held in a prison or remand centre until a place became available. Until the opening of the first remand centre at Ashford in 1961 there was frequent questioning in the House of Commons over the delay in implementing the 1948 Act; since 1961 questions in the House regarding centres have been almost wholly taken up with the shortfall in their provision. It has clearly become a basic expectation in British penal practice that no unsentenced person under 21 years of age should be housed in a local prison. And that very expectation has contributed to the present plight of the remand centres. Once remand centres were built it became increasingly difficult to place young unsentenced persons in local prisons where they soon constituted a declining minority. Indeed the Prison Department was so anxious to demonstrate that unsentenced persons under 21 years had been largely removed from the local prisons that as early as 1965 it announced that 80 per cent of the average daily population of all remand prisoners under 21 years of age (716 persons out of 893) were in remand centres (Cmnd 3088, 1966). With the steady growth of remands in custody for this age group since then there has been no acceptable alternative to coping with this increase but doubling up in the existing centres.

This concern becomes more understandable when one considers that much of the increase in the remand population under 21 years is accounted for by the dramatic growth in numbers of those in the very youngest group held in Prison Department establishments. Between 1960 and 1972 the number of receptions of untried and unsentenced persons under 17 years of age increased by at least 400 per cent. It is not possible to be sure, because apart from the usual difficulty that the same person may be received more than once in the same category, in 1960 the statistics did not distinguish between the reception of untried and unsentenced persons (Cmnd 1467, 1961, Table 612), whereas in 1972 separate figures were published for

these two groups. In 1960 there were 515 receptions of which 18
were for girls: in 1972 there were 2,066 receptions of untried
persons under 17 years of which 91 were for girls, and 2041 receptions of unsentenced persons including 83 for girls (Cmnd 5489,
1973, Table C12). Receptions under the age of 17 accounted for 6
per cent of all receptions for untried and unsentenced prisoners in
1972, and for 15.4 per cent of those receptions in the under 21 age
group. Assuming that the average duration of custody for untried
and unsentenced prisoners does not vary with age, there were probably about 250 young persons under the age of 17 years in the prison
system at any one time in 1972, most of them presumably in remand
centres.

It was not until 1972 that the annual Statistical Tables published by the Prison Department (Cmnd 5489, 1973) provided, for the
first time, an analysis of the average daily population by type of
penal institution. On the basis of this information we have estimated in Table 2.4 the nature and distribution of the daily population in 1960, the year before the first remand centre came into
operation, and 1968 in order to assess the degree to which the population accommodated in different types of establishments has changed
in recent years. In doing so we have assumed that the proportion of
civil, untried, unsentenced and borstal trainee prisoners held in
remand centres, local and training prisons was the same in 1968 as
in 1972. Clearly this may not have been the case, but since the
contribution which these groups make to the average daily population
of local and training prisons is so small, the overall picture will
not have been unduly affected. It should also be noted that our
category of training prisons would have included in 1960 what were
then called central prisons and corrective training prisons; and
that some of the open prisons which are today classed as training
prisons were then classed as special local prisons. This should not
affect the comparisons except in the case of civil prisoners, many
of whom were probably housed in the special locals in 1960. Rather
than include all civil prisoners in the local prison category,
therefore, which would be technically correct but somewhat misleading, we have in Table 2.4 distributed them between the locals and
the training prisons in the same proportions as for 1972. Table 2.5
presents these estimates as proportions of the different categories
of prisoner which made up the daily average population in remand
centres, local prisons and training prisons for 1960, 1968 and 1972.

The population of remand centres is almost wholly composed of untried and unsentenced prisoners, although a sizeable minority, some
9 per cent, are sentenced persons. The latter are not merely
borstal trainees or sentenced prisoners awaiting transfer: some
remand centres for men house young prisoners, and some for women accommodate young and adult prisoners, on a more permanent basis as
domestic or maintenance workers. Without the remand centres, of
course, the pressure of population in the local prisons would be
worse than it is, but it is clear from Table 2.5 that the introduction of remand centres has done nothing to reduce the overall
burden of untried and unsentenced prisoners in the population of the
locals: in 1960 they accounted for 12.1 per cent and in 1972 for
18.0 per cent. In recent years the rate of increase in untried and
unsentenced prisoners in the population of the locals has been

TABLE 2.4 Estimated daily average population of males and females in different legal categories contained in remand centres, locals and training prisons for 1960, 1968 and 1972

	1960		1968			1972		
	Local prison	Train. prison	Rem. centre	Local prison	Train. prison	Rem. centre	Local prison	Train. prison
Untried under 21	414	–	488	123	–	719	182	–
over 21	1,018	–	205	1,119	–	307	1,650	–
Unsentenced under 21	286	–	452	105	–	717	167	–
over 21	367	–	113	550	–	162	791	–
Civil prisoners	342	51	16	400	61	22	412	63
Sentenced adults	14,092	4,736	40	10,316	9,965	59	11,613	12,862
YPs	412	596	69	478	557	94	644	615
Borstal trainees	223	–	59	204	–	35	122	–
Totals	17,154	5,383	1,442	13,295	10,583	2,115	15,581	13,540

Note: The figures for 1972 are derived from Table E.2 in the 1972 Prison Department Statistical Tables (Cmnd 5489) with a single modification. In the Prison Dept Statistics the adult section of Risley Remand Centre has been included with the figures for local prisons. Taking population data from Appendix No.3 of the Report on the Prison Department for 1972 (Cmnd 5375), and making the assumption that the proportions of adult untried and unsentenced prisoners in Risley are the same as in the prison population as a whole, figures for adults in Risley Remand Centre have been estimated and included with remand centres.

The figures for 1968 are estimates since Table E.2 in the 1968 Prison Dept Statistical Tables (Cmnd 4266) does not include a breakdown of the population by type of prison. Total numbers of prisoners on average held in different institutions are derived from Appendix No.3 of the Report on the Prison Dept for 1968 (Cmnd 4186) and total numbers of prisoners by legal category held in all institutions from the Summary of Reception and Population figures for 1968 included in the Statistical Tables (Cmnd 4266). In making estimates it was assumed that the proportion of untried, unsentenced, civil and borstal trainee prisoners held in the different establishments was the same as in 1972.

The figures for 1960 have similarly been derived from the information contained in the summary of Reception and Population, and Appendix 4 of the Report on the Prison Department for 1960 (Cmnd 1467) and from Table E.2 of the Statistical Tables for that year (Cmnd 1467).

TABLE 2.5 Estimated proportions of males and females in different legal categories contained in remand centres, local and training prisons for 1960, 1968 and 1972

	1960		1968			1972		
	Local prison	Train. prison	Rem. centre	Local prison	Train. prison	Rem. centre	Local prison	Train. prison
Untried under 21	2.4	0.0	33.8	0.9	0.0	34.0	1.2	0.0
over 21	5.9	0.0	14.2	8.4	0.0	14.5	10.6	0.0
Unsentenced under 21	1.7	0.0	31.4	0.8	0.0	33.9	1.1	0.0
over 21	2.1	0.0	7.8	4.1	0.0	7.7	5.1	0.0
Civil prisoners	1.9	1.0	1.1	3.0	0.6	1.0	2.6	0.5
Sentenced adults	82.2	88.0	2.8	77.6	94.2	2.8	74.5	95.0
YPs	2.4	11.1	4.8	3.6	5.3	4.4	4.1	4.5
Borstal trainees	1.3	0.0	4.1	1.5	0.0	1.7	0.8	0.0
Totals	100.0	100.0	100.0	100.0	100.0	100.0	100.0	100.0

Note: For the way in which estimates were derived see note to Table 2.4.

faster than that of sentenced prisoners - in 1972 the former were 47
per cent up on 1968 compared to 12 per cent for the latter. In
spite of their relative smallness as a group compared to sentenced
prisoners they accounted for two-fifths of the total increase in the
population in local prisons during those years. It is true that the
proportionate contribution to the population of local prisons made
by young untried and unsentenced persons is smaller now than it was
in 1960. But it is also true that this contribution has gone up
quite markedly, both absolutely and proportionately, since 1968.
Nearly one in every five of all untried and unsentenced prisoners
under 21 years was still being accommodated in local prisons in
1972. Regrettably the data provided by the Prison Department in the
Statistical Tables do not enable us to say how many of these are
under 17 years. If these younger persons were distributed between
institutions in the same way as their older counterparts then, in
1972, we could have expected perhaps as many as fifty of them to be
in the local prisons at any one time. No doubt the special efforts
made by the Home Office to keep the very young out of prison, have
kept the numbers much below that figure on average. Even so in June
1974 there were thirty such persons held in adult prisons ('The
Times', 24 July 1974).
   The development of training prisons on the other hand has, of
course, taken up much of the increase in numbers of sentenced
prisoners over the years. It has also effected some decline in the
burden of this group, both absolutely and as a proportion of the
population, in the local prisons since 1960: there was an absolute
reduction of 2,247 sentenced prisoners (excluding civil prisoners
and borstal trainees) on average in 1972 compared to 1960 and these
accounted for 6 per cent less of the total population in local
prisons. In other words, the proportion of all sentenced prisoners
who were housed in the local prisons declined from 73.1 per cent in
1960 to 50.4 per cent in 1968 and 47.4 per cent in 1972. The re-
ductions were clearly more marked up to 1968 since when the position
has changed. Over the period 1968 to 1972 there was in fact an increase in the numbers of both sentenced adults and young prisoners
held in the local prisons. While the increase for sentenced adults
was overshadowed by that of untried and unsentenced prisoners, so
that they continued to decline as a proportion of the population in
the locals, the increase in young prisoners was such as to increase
their relative contribution to the work of the local prisons.
Indeed in 1972 there were actually more young prisoners in the local
prisons than in the training prisons. There was a slight increase
in the numbers of civil prisoners held in local prisons, the fall in
some categories being more than offset by the rising numbers of illegal Commonwealth immigrants since 1969, but they have declined
relative to other groups in the population of all types of establishment including the local prisons. Only in the case of
borstal trainees awaiting transfer have both numbers and their proportionate contribution to the population in local prisons actually
declined over the period since 1968. And this, of course, has
nothing to do with the provision of training prisons, nor for that
matter of more borstal places, but results from greater rational-
isation of the borstal allocation procedures.
   In spite of these changes the overriding impression to be gained

is that the condition of the local prisons is remarkably little
different from what it was in Fox's day. The local prison is still
an institution performing multiple functions for several groups of
prisoners which, if anything, are tending to become more equally
represented in the population. The local prisons thus remain in a
special dilemma. If, as Sparks suggests, they are in a state of
crisis because they have to contain too many prisoners, then that
crisis is greatly exacerbated by the rapid increase in numbers of
prisoners who have not yet been sentenced to imprisonment. But if,
as the White Paper 'People in Prison' suggests, the first duty of
the local prisons is to the courts by dealing with trials and
remands, then they have to discharge this duty at the same time that
they cope with a particularly difficult mixture of sentenced prisoners among whom unskilled recidivists greatly predominate. Indeed
those who might wish to argue that 'neighbourhood' prisons of the
kind discussed in the previous chapter could not cope with the more
serious offenders would do well to reflect on the composition of the
existing locals. Only about one in twenty-five of the sentenced
population in local prisons is there in default of payment of a fine
and the proportion has been steadily declining following the Criminal Justice Act 1967. In 1972 51.6 per cent of those in the local
prisons under sentence were serving eighteen months or less, while
38.4 per cent were serving sentences of more than eighteen months to
four years and 10 per cent sentences of more than four years including life (Cmnd 5489, 1973, Table E.2). And while according to
Sparks' (1971) estimates some two-thirds of all these were convicted
of breaking offences or larceny, about half of the remainder were
convicted of sexual or violent offences.
    It should be noted, of course, that not all of the twenty-four
local prisons will have the same distribution of prisoners in their
populations. Among the London locals, for example, there is a
degree of specialisation so that Brixton takes all the untried
prisoners in addition to sentenced prisoners, while Wandsworth and
Pentonville take the convicted but unsentenced; and in the north of
England, the opening of Risley Remand Centre has relieved Manchester
and Liverpool local prisons of the need to take any prisoners on
remand. Nevertheless the figures in Tables 2.4 and 2.5 probably
give a fair guide to the tasks confronting our overcrowded provincial locals.

Chapter 3

HM PRISON WINCHESTER

At the beginning of March 1971 we embarked on a three month period
of fieldwork at Winchester local prison and Winchester remand centre
as part of the Prison Regimes Project. HM Prison Winchester is the
largest, in terms of its population if not its certified accommodation, of the eight local prisons in the South West Region.
Nationally it comes next in size after the four London locals and
the five major provincial prisons at Birmingham, Durham, Leeds,
Liverpool and Manchester. The oldest of our current stock of local
prisons was brought into use in 1795 and the newest in 1892:
Winchester was rebuilt in 1846 to replace the old County Gaol. Like
so many of our prisons it was designed to hold prisoners in the
Pennsylvania system of separate confinement in single cells arranged
along the landings of five wings which radiate outwards from the
'centre' like the spokes of a wheel. At the time of our study
prisoners were accommodated on the three upper landings (known as
the 'twos', 'threes' and 'fours') of each of four wings A,B,C and D
which then provided 138, 207, 235 and 149 beds respectively. About
three-quarters of the beds were in triple cells - that is cells,
13 ft 6 in. long by 7 ft 6 in. wide by 8 ft 6 in. high. Each of
these cells typically contained two bunks and a bed, two washstands,
two tables and three chairs, and very little else. Floor space in a
triple cell was thus 34 square feet per person. About one-sixth of
the beds were in single cells of the same dimensions which thus
yielded 101 square feet for the occupant. The remainder were in
dormitories, known as 'grade rooms', for between five and seven
prisoners. These had each been converted from two cells with an adjacent toilet recess constructed from a third. The grade rooms were
better fitted than the cells but provided only 31 square feet for
each of seven persons or 43 square feet if the room were occupied by
five persons. With up to four bunks and three beds in them they
looked rather crowded. There were no double cells in Winchester at
the time of our study. The last wing, E wing, was used for administrative offices. The basements (the 'ones') had a variety of uses:
A wing housed the punishment block; C wing the segregation unit for
prisoners on Rule 43; and B,D and E wings the stores, central
kitchens and the prison dog section.
Although workshops had been added to the prison over the years

and most of the cells had been refurbished by the time of our fieldwork, the basic structure of the main prison has remained much the
same for a century and a quarter. Two features of Winchester's comparatively recent history are still discernible today. The laundry
stalls in No.7 workshop, the separate exercise yards and the
separate entrances to the chapel bear testimony to the days when
Winchester accommodated women prisoners as well as men. And the
sensibilities which led to the location of staff rather than prisoners in the converted cells which take up much of one side of the
ground floor on D wing serves as a constant reminder of the time
when Winchester, like other locals in the days of capital punishment, was a hanging prison. The last few years have seen the opening of a purpose built remand centre for male persons under 21 as an
annexe to the rear of the prison (and which will be discussed in
detail in chapter 4) and the erection of a new building adjoining A
wing which provides reception, educational, recreational and further
visiting facilities. These, together with the paraphernalia of
post-Mountbatten security, are the main physical manifestations of
the penal philosophy of the second half of the twentieth century.

At the time of our fieldwork Winchester received prisoners from
courts in three counties: from the whole of Hampshire and the Isle
of Wight, with the exception of Bournemouth Borough from which adult
prisoners went to HMP Dorchester; from eastern Wiltshire as far as
Salisbury, with the exception of Salisbury County Quarter Sessions;
and from southern Berkshire as far as Newbury but excluding the
Newbury County Quarter Sessions jurisdiction. In addition some
prisoners were received on transfer from other prisons for accumulated visits, for diagnosis and treatment in the hospital, for production at court, or for other administrative reasons such as their
unsuitability for the prisons to which they had been allocated. The
size of Winchester's catchment area is reflected in the fact that
the mean distance from next of kin for married men in our sample was
49 miles. Prisoners received at Winchester could, of course, be assigned to any security category and part of the prison's function
was to decide the security class of prisoners sent there.

In 1971 there were on average 16 or 17 receptions daily and a
similar number of discharges. Over the year the prison received
2,672 untried prisoners, 108 civil prisoners, and 2,274 convicted
prisoners though most of the latter were not in fact receptions
under sentence.

An untried prisoner would normally be remanded in custody for
periods of not more than eight clear days at a time. However, if he
was waiting to appear before a higher court the time spent in custody might vary between a few days and several months depending on the
timing and calendar of the courts, and the outcome of any application for release on bail. Untried prisoners, known as 'trials and
remands', were located, together with civil prisoners, on the
'threes' and 'fours' of A wing which was the former women's section
of the prison. The accommodation on these landings provided 20
places in single cells and 69 in triple cells.

Convicted but unsentenced prisoners were usually received under
sections 14,20,28, or 29 of the Magistrates' Court Act 1952 and
sections 41 or 56 of the Criminal Justice Act 1967. Sometimes
prisoners were received under other provisions, such as sections 6

or 8 of the Criminal Justice Act 1948 and section 23 of the Children and Young Persons Act 1969. They were collectively known within Winchester as 'section prisoners' or simply 'sections' and for the most part were not separately housed but could be found on the same landings with sentenced prisoners in B,C and D wings and the ground floor of A wing. Occasionally prisoners on whom the Bench had chosen to respite judgment might be located with the trial and remand prisoners, and prisoners received under section 26 of the Magistrates' Courts Act 1952 for medical reports would normally be placed in the prison hospital. Persons remanded for reports requested by the courts would normally be in custody for periods up to twenty-one days, but again for those awaiting appearance at higher courts the period could vary considerably.

Sentenced prisoners attended a reception Board on the day after arrival which allocated them to one of two induction workshops. In theory 'stars' - that is prisoners undergoing their first sentence of imprisonment or whom the authorities deemed could be treated as such - went to No.5 Shop and recidivists to Shop No.4: in either case the work was the same - the manufacture and repair of mailbags. The induction period lasted approximately four weeks and during that time, or most of it, the prisoner was located on B wing. The prisoner would be lodged in any available vacant cell subject to the following considerations: sick and disabled prisoners were normally 'located flat' on B2 thereby avoiding the need to climb stairs and being within easy reach of staff; sex offenders were usually given single cells on B3 or B4; and prisoners with escape histories (E list men) or who were otherwise seen as security risks were placed in special cells with red doors on B3. Young prisoners awaiting transfer to Young Prisoner training establishments were allocated to work in Shop No.7 on mattress assembly and were housed on B4 either in small dormitories or in cells.

The career of sentenced prisoners then depended on several factors; most notably length of sentence, security classification and previous prison experience. Prisoners serving three months to three years were considered by an internal review board within three to six weeks of arrival. The review board settled the security category of each prisoner and, subject to South West Regional Office confirmation, allocated him either to remain in Winchester or to be transferred to another prison to serve his sentence. Most frequently transfers were to The Verne, Halden Camp or Ford, and for Rule 43 prisoners who had to be kept separate from other prisoners either for their own protection or for other reasons to Shepton Mallet; but transfers to a number of other prisons also occurred. Prisoners coming before the review board were reallocated to labour and moved to C and D wings. In practice many prisoners were reassigned to C or D wings before their review board because it was prison policy to keep these wings full to leave room for new receptions. High security Category A prisoners and E list prisoners were again housed in security cells: this time in red cells which 'faced the cage' - the fenced exercise area between the two wings. Prisoners serving less than three months were not eligible for review, and at times under the pressure of numbers prisoners serving rather longer than that were not in fact reviewed. These prisoners were considered for change of labour on application and would be moved to different locations depending on the time left to serve at the end of the induction period.

Long sentence prisoners did not come before the review board but were dealt with in one of two ways. Recidivists serving three to five years, and stars serving three to four years, were allocated by South West Regional Office on the basis of documents prepared at Winchester. Recidivists serving five years or longer and stars serving four years or longer would be transferred along with preliminary documentation to Bristol Prison, where they would be further observed and dealt with by the Long-Term Allocation Board. In theory long term prisoners were transferred from Winchester after four to six weeks; but whereas during 1970 and 1971 it was easy to find places for recidivists serving three to four years, usually at Dartmoor, and for persons suitable for open conditions, it was more difficult to find vacancies for long term prisoners in closed prisons. During our research at Winchester delays of more than six months before prisoners could be transferred to the Long-Term Allocation Centre were the rule rather than the exception. It was similarly difficult to transfer Category B Rule 43 prisoners; and the problem of finding accommodation for young prisoners in the appropriate establishments was often solved by the expedient of reclassifying them as adults.

TABLE 3.1 Average daily population in HMP Winchester and estimate for all local prisons 1971

	HMP Winchester		Estimate for all locals
	No.	%	%
Untried prisoners	63	10.1	10.8
Unsentenced prisoners	34	5.5	4.6
Sentenced adults	501	80.6	76.1
Sentenced YPs	3	0.5	4.9
Civil prisoners	19	3.1	2.7
Borstal trainees	1	0.2	0.9
Totals	621	100.0	100.0

Note: The estimates for all local prisons have been derived as described in the note to Table 2.4.

During 1970 the average daily population at Winchester was higher than it had been for any year during the previous decade and it remained at this level throughout 1971. Table 3.1 gives the average numbers and proportions in each class of prisoner at Winchester in 1971 (as supplied to us by Prison Department), together with our estimated proportions for local prisons as a whole. According to these estimates Winchester closely resembled the average population for local prisons and can thus be said to be fairly typical at least of provincial locals.

Our work at Winchester was designed as part of a wider study to discover the different regimes which might be experienced in different types of prison. Given the heterogeneous population of a local prison, however, we hoped in spite of our small resources to learn at least something of the regimes for different categories of prisoner within Winchester. To do this we interviewed Principal Officers or Senior Officers about the routine in the wings for which they were responsible, and also a sample of prisoners about the routine as it was perceived to apply to them. We used a series of schedules which we had developed after a long period of preliminary work in other prisons. We checked prisoner responses against staff responses and against our own observations during the course of the fieldwork. Since the questions we asked were largely factual, and the answers easily verifiable, there was a high degree of agreement. Most of the data reported in this paper are taken from the information supplied by prisoners, but we have not included anything the authenticity of which we could find any reason to question.

We expected that regimes might differ according to the legal status of the prisoners, their location within the prison and the work they were required to do. Because of the length of time involved in interviewing, and the high turnover of prisoners through receptions, discharges and internal transfers from wing to wing, it was decided to sample bed spaces on each landing within the prison according to the distribution of prisoners on a given date at the beginning of the research. Occupants of sampled beds were then approached for interview if they came within the status categories for which quota samples were required. Finally no person was interviewed who expressed unwillingness to take part. In the event all but one prisoner agreed to participate and few substitutes were necessary because cell use had changed. Only small numbers of civil prisoners were to be found in the population at any one time and all cell spaces occupied by civil prisoners on the sample date were included to ensure the representation of this group. Because of limited resources, and the large number of separate jobs performed by prisoners, it was not possible for the sampling procedures to take account of occupations, except in so far as occupation to some degree determined cell allocations. The hospital was excluded from the study, partly because the prison authorities requested it on grounds of the inconvenience the research would have caused, and partly because its inclusion would have unnecessarily complicated our research design and added to the considerable burden of fieldwork. Prisoners on punishment and those on Rule 43 were excluded for the same reasons. The resulting sample and the population of the prison on 4 March 1971, the sample date, are given in Table 3.2.

The sentenced prisoners in the sample included a high proportion of serious recidivist offenders serving comparatively long sentences (cf.Sparks, 1971). More than half were rated in security category B and had committed Class 1 offences against the person or Class 2 offences against property with violence: three-fifths had been in prison before and about a third of those had served more than five previous sentences totalling over six years; nearly two-fifths were serving between one and two years and more than a third had sentences longer than two years. On the other hand about two-fifths had committed less serious offences, were rated in security category

C, had no previous experience of imprisonment and were serving less than one year.

TABLE 3.2   HMP Winchester — Population on 4 March 1971 and sample selected

	Population 4 March 1971	Sample
Untried prisoners	52	10
Unsentenced prisoners	12*	
Sentenced adults	518	50
Sentenced YPs	14	
Civil prisoners	5	5
Totals	601	65

* It was decided not to sample prisoners held in the hospital, nor those on punishment or in special accommodation under Rule 43. The figure for unsentenced prisoners is lower than the average daily population for this group quoted in Table 3.1 because many of them were housed in the hospital awaiting medical reports under Section 26 of the Magistrates' Courts Act 1952.

Before we present our findings on the day-to-day regimes at Winchester it will probably be helpful at this point if we review some of the formal provisions applying to the various special classes of prisoner in the system and the extent to which these were or could have been put into practice at Winchester. Contemporary prison management is governed by the Prison Act 1952 (section 47) which states that:
  The Secretary of State may make rules for the regulation and management of prisons, remand centres, detention centres and Borstal institutions respectively, and for the classification, treatment, employment, discipline and control of persons required to be detained therein.
  The rules formulated by the Secretary of State and which were current during the period of the research are contained in the statutory instruments The Prison Rules 1964 (SI no.388) and The Prison (Amendment) Rules 1968 (SI no.440). The 1964 Rules distinguish between convicted prisoners and unconvicted prisoners for several purposes. They do not distinguish between those convicted prisoners who are sentenced and those who are unsentenced except in so far as Rule 62 protects the rights of the latter to visits, medical examinations and letters in relation to any court proceedings. In Winchester during the course of our research in 1971 we observed no systematic differences in the daily management of these groups of prisoners and no one reported any such differences to us. As far as we were able to ascertain from our discussions with staff a distinction was maintained only to ensure that the unsentenced were produced for sentence at the appropriate time and the sentenced for review and allocation. It is probable that those 'sections' who

were housed in the hospital during the preparation of medical
reports for the courts experienced a rather different regime, though
not necessarily a more flexible or rewarding one. Indeed we were
informed by hospital staff that the regime in the hospital was designed so that prisoners might be available to the medical staff at
any time. Thus apart from two half-hour periods of exercise their
time was spent either in hospital cells or wards when they were not
actually being interviewed or undergoing treatment. One or two
prisoners were given 'occupational therapy' in the hospital; otherwise no work was available to hospital residents. Those unsentenced
prisoners housed in the main prison had no special allocation of
space, and, as we have already noted, could be found on the same
landings with sentenced prisoners. The findings reported later in
relation to the group of sentenced prisoners who were not eligible
for association may therefore be taken to apply equally to convicted
persons not yet sentenced and housed in the main prison.

The Prison Rules as they apply to civil prisoners represent a
sort of compromise between the treatment of untried prisoners and
convicted prisoners. Under Rule 3 they are to be treated as a separate class of prisoner, although under Rule 63(2) they may associate
with other prisoners if they wish. Like unconvicted prisoners they
may wear their own clothes and may have unrestricted letters and
visits subject to the conditions of Rules 20(1) and 34(1) which we
discuss below. In other respects they are treated in the same way
as convicted prisoners. Although additional privileges apply to
certain other special categories of civil prisoner, these were not
represented in the population at Winchester while we were there. In
so far as it was possible to judge that civil prisoners experienced
a separate regime, given the small numbers in the population at the
time, we report that regime as well in the paragraphs below.

Two countervailing principles of jurisprudence and one from penology seem to underpin the special provisions made for unconvicted
persons in custody. First, unconvicted prisoners must be presumed
to be innocent. As such it is inappropriate that they should be
punished, or that they should be detained with convicted persons, or
that they should be deprived of any rights that pertain to non-
accused persons other than those losses inherent in the process of
detention itself. This view has been endorsed at least since the
Prison Act of 1877 which provided for Rules for the unconvicted to
make their confinement 'as little as possible oppressive'. The 1964
Prison Rules distinguish between the unconvicted and the convicted,
to protect the rights of the former, on nine separate occasions:

Rule 3(2)   provides that unconvicted prisoners 'shall be kept
              out of contact with convicted prisoners as far as
              this can reasonably be done'.

Rule 17(4)   provides that an unconvicted prisoner may have the
              services of his own doctor or dentist, providing
              there are reasonable grounds, and at his own expense.

Rule 20(1)   provides that 'an unconvicted prisoner may wear
              clothing of his own if and in so far as it is
              suitable, tidy and clean'.

Rule 21(1)   provides that 'an unconvicted prisoner may be supplied with food at his own expense, or that of his friends'.

Rule 25   states that the 'governor or visiting committee or board of visitors, may on application by an unconvicted prisoner, permit him on payment of a sum fixed by the Secretary of State -
a) to occupy a room or cell specially fitted for such prisoners and provided with suitable bedding and other articles in addition to, or different from, those ordinarily provided, and to have at his own expense the use of private furniture and utensils approved by the governor and
b) to be relieved of the duty of cleaning his room or cell and similar duties.'

Rule 26(2)   provides 'that an unconvicted prisoner shall not be required to have his hair cut or beard or moustache usually worn by him shaved off except where the Medical Officer directs this to be done for the sake of health or cleanliness'.

Rule 28(5)   states that 'an unconvicted prisoner may be permitted, if he wishes, to work as if he were a convicted prisoner' and in doing so guarantees his right not to work if he so chooses.

Rule 34(1)   provides that 'an unconvicted prisoner may send and receive as many letters and may receive as many visits as he wishes'.

Rule 41(1)   states that 'an unconvicted prisoner may have supplied to him at his expense and retain for his own use books, newspapers, writing materials and other means of occupation'.

Certain other Rules, without specifying unconvicted prisoners, none the less provide protection for them as well as others in respect of appearances at court, the finding of sureties and payments of debts and fines.

The presumption of innocence, however, on which these provisions are based is tempered by a second principle, namely, that the course of justice must proceed unhindered by the activities of those who would seek to subvert it. Somewhat artlessly in 1957 Elkin could write that since the prison 'authorities must act on the assumption that the courts would not have remanded in custody if it had been wise or safe to leave those particular individuals at large' then 'it is the duty of the prison authorities to see that nothing happens to defeat the ends of justice, and therefore there must be some degree of constraint whether this is compatible with the presumption of innocence or not' (Elkin, 1957, p.120). Such a view was also propounded by Sir Lionel Fox in respect of untried prisoners whom he had come to regard as an 'awkward anomaly' within the prison system. With what seems stunning complacency, given that in 1952 well over two-fifths of those remanded were not returned to custody on sentence and probably many more than that had not been in custody

before, Fox wrote 'that the majority of these prisoners, whether or
no they have committed the offences currently charged, are not in
fact respectable and innocent persons but old hands well known to
the prison staffs' (Fox, 1952, pp.285-6).

It is not entirely clear what particular restraints Elkin and Fox
saw as necessary, although sufficient regulations were incorporated
in the standing orders and circular instructions of the then Prison
Commission for Fox to conclude that 'the lot of an untried prisoner
may seem in practice to be more depressing, even if "less oppressive" than that of the convicted prisoner' (Fox, 1952, p.286).
The separation of unconvicted from convicted prisoners under Rule 3,
of course, serves well to prevent any conspiracy to evade justice
that was envisaged in the Prison Act of 1877. And the general sus-
picion of guilt deriving from this second principle presumably goes
a long way to account for the lack of enthusiasm with which the
rights of the unconvicted are publicly promoted.

The separation of the unconvicted from the convicted receives
further support from a basic principle of penology: that the innocent, or at least the less well versed in prison culture, should be
protected from contamination by the more criminally sophisticated.
Indeed the special Rules of 1877 were as concerned to forestall such
contamination as they were to prevent conspiracy.

But it may well be the case that the functional importance of
separating the unconvicted from the convicted lies not so much in
the protection afforded to the former, as in the preservation of the
social order that is established between convicted prisoners and the
staff. The participants in the prison social system are divided
into two groups: the prisoners who stand morally condemned, found
guilty by due process of law, and the staff whose moral rectitude,
since they are entrusted with the administration of the sentence of
the court, has been publicly proclaimed. In this context the unconvicted prisoner is 'an awkward anomaly', a potentially disruptive
influence whose moral status is as yet in doubt. The public exercise of his legal privileges with their appeal to the standards of
the outside world, serves to point up the temporary nature of imprisonment, the intrusiveness of its rules and the tenuous balance
of power that sustains them.

In any case the practicalities of the situation demand, as Fox
(1952) noted, that whatever special rules are created for unconvicted prisoners, 'they must be applied in, and be compatible
with the regime of, an establishment primarily designed for and
populated by convicted prisoners' (p.285). Thus apart from the
special Rules outlined above, untried prisoners are subject to the
same general Rules and discipline as convicted prisoners. And with
the exception of the right not to work and the rights in respect of
those letters and visits which affect bail or defence considerations, all the special provisions are subject in one way or another
to revocation by the governor, the medical officer, the Visiting
Committee as it then was or the Board of Visitors, and the Secretary
of State.

Perhaps we should begin our discussion of the situation of unconvicted prisoners in Winchester by describing the attempt made to
keep them out of contact with convicted men in accordance with Rule
3(2). Complete separation was not possible given the design of the

prison and the meagre facilities available; and it might be thought
that the very high degree of separation which was attained was
achieved at great cost. The prison had no special vehicles of its
own and receptions were brought to Winchester either by the police
or in such private transport as could be arranged. Prisoners were
closely supervised but in such circumstances the separation of
different categories of prisoner could not be guaranteed. Sometimes
further problems were encountered on arrival at the prison. Although the new building adjoining A wing was designed to facilitate
the smooth passage of both unconvicted and convicted prisoners
through the reception process without mixing, too few waiting
'boxes' had been provided so that at busy periods a certain amount
of contact between categories was unavoidable. Inside the main
prison the radial design meant that virtually all movements involved
prisoners passing through 'the centre': movements of unconvicted
prisoners to work, visits, appointments and exercise could thus provide opportunities for contact with any of the convicted prisoners
who were usually to be found, as in most busy locals, working as
cleaners or orderlies or who for some other legitimate reason were
out of their cells.

None the less a very substantial degree of separation between the
different classes of prisoner was most effectively achieved by the
simple expedient of keeping unconvicted prisoners locked in their
cells for the greater part of the day. The typical weekday time-
table for remand prisoners in A wing was as follows:

Time	Activity
07.00–07.30	Unlocked for slopping out, collecting water for washing and collecting breakfast.
07.30–08.50	Locked in cell - breakfast, washing.
08.50–09.30	Unlocked for exercise on parade ground.
09.30–12.00	Locked in cell.
12.00–12.10	Unlocked for collecting midday meal.
12.10–14.00	Locked in cell - midday meal.
14.00–14.30	Unlocked for exercise on parade ground.
14.30–17.00	Locked in cell.
17.00–17.10	Unlocked for collecting tea.
17.10–19.10	Locked in cell - tea.
19.10–19.15	Unlocked for slopping out, cocoa delivered to cell.
19.15–07.00	Locked in cell for night.

Unconvicted prisoners were permitted no periods of association
even with each other – unless one counts the association that was
enforced on up to 77 per cent of them who had to share three to a
cell when the available accommodation was fully stretched. The remaining 23 per cent in such circumstances would be kept virtually in
solitary confinement, although usually, when there was less pressure
on places, rather more would be in this state. In either case the
rider to Rule 3(3) which says 'Nothing in this Rule shall require a
prisoner to be deprived unduly of the society of other persons' has
an ironic ring. Unconvicted prisoners normally had no facilities
for watching television and no opportunity to attend evening educational or physical training classes. Thus, if the prisoner chose
not to work, and leaving aside any visits or special appointments
with staff that he might have, he left his cell only for exercise,

for collecting his meals and for satisfying the minimum requirements
of hygiene. If the prisoner chose to work he enjoyed some degree of
contact with, or contamination from, other prisoners with whom he
was employed and he considerably reduced the amount of time during
which he was 'banged up'. At weekends no work was available, but
remand and trial prisoners could take their turn to attend the
weekly film show in the gymnasium if they wished. Even so the mean
daily time spent locked in cells reported by our sample of unconvicted men was 21 hours and 40 minutes - a good deal longer than
that for the majority of convicted men.

All convicted prisoners were required to work provided that they
were fit to do so and that work was available for them. About
three-fifths were employed in workshops - the majority making or
repairing mailbags and the remainder engaged in laundry work and the
tailoring trades. About one-third were employed on the various domestic and maintenance parties servicing the prison, and one group
travelled some thirty miles daily to tend the gardens of the Police
College. A few prisoners were occupied on trade training and, even
when the shops were fully operational, about one in twenty prisoners
would be unemployed for various reasons. A prisoner's occupation to
some degree determined the location of his cell and the amount of
time he might spend in it. But for most convicted prisoners time in
cells was a function of whether or not one was permitted to 'dine
out' in association and to participate in recreational activities
which was in turn dependent on the 'stage' of sentence reached.
Prisoners who had served one-third of a sentence of six months or
longer could apply to dine out. If their application was successful
they were unlocked in the wing during weekdays between 12 noon and
14.00 and again from 17.00 to 20.00. Because of the very restricted
space available - less than 47 square feet of floor space for every
bed in the cells - there was a waiting list for dining out, and in
practice hardly any prisoners serving less than one year enjoyed
this privilege. Prisoners who were not eligible or not permitted
to dine out, ate in cells and apart from transient meetings during
washing or collecting meals could associate with other prisoners
only at work, at educational and physical training classes and at
chapel. At weekends only those prisoners essential to the mainte-
.nance of the prison worked, and there was no freedom of association.
Nearly all prisoners were permitted by turns to watch the weekly
film and television on Saturday and Sunday afternoons. During the
week the mean time spent in cells for the convicted prisoners in our
sample was approximately 15 hours; at weekends it rose to 19 hours.

In these circumstances the statutory provisions which we have
outlined for the unconvicted prisoners could be expected to take on
a special importance, offering as they do a chance to relieve the
tedium at least. How far were they put into effect at Winchester?

THE RIGHT TO HAVE PRIVATE MEDICAL ATTENTION

None of the prisoners in our sample had received private medical
services, and it is only fair to say that none reported that they
would have wanted them.

THE RIGHT TO WEAR OWN CLOTHES

Most unconvicted men received at Winchester, as at other local
prisons, arrived with only the clothes they were wearing at the time
of arrest. Whether or not they retained them was dependent on the
judgment of the reception officer in accordance with Rule 20(1).
Some prisoners were required to wear prison clothing immediately on
arrival. In making such a decision, we were told, the reception
officer 'uses his common sense' but he 'doesn't allow a man to go
into the main prison unsuitably dressed'. Unless the prisoner had
friends or relatives who were willing and able to provide a change
of under-clothing he was dependent on prison supply during launder-
ing. And since, under Standing Order 2(c)6, only private under-
clothing and not outer clothing may be laundered in the prison,
those in custody for long periods had to resort to prison clothing
because they were unable to obtain replacements from outside. It
should be noted that at the time of our study the South West Regional Reception and Discharge sub-committee had made recommendations
for the provision of launderette and pressing facilities for remand
prisoners. But the fact remains that half of the unconvicted
prisoners we interviewed were wearing prison 'browns' - the uniform
supplied to distinguish them from convicted prisoners who wore
'greys' - and only two of the remainder were fully dressed in their
own clothes. None of the five civil prisoners in our sample was
wearing his own clothes. Had they chosen to do so they would have
been required to work in cells - which would have involved something
approaching solitary confinement.

THE RIGHT TO HAVE FOOD SENT IN

The Rule regarding the sending in of food seems simple enough. However, apart from the fact that few prisoners had either the financial or social resources to arrange for such supplies, the interpretation of the Rule in Standing Order 2(b)5 created additional
difficulties. Meals could be ordered by the prisoner, or be sent in
by his friends, but only if they were 'full' meals, that is if they
completely replaced a prison meal. Alcohol of certain kinds and in
strictly limited quantities, or other drinks, were only accepted 'as
part of a meal'. Supplementary articles of food such as 'choco-
lates, sweets, fresh fruit and shelled nuts in reasonable quantities' could be sent in by friends and relatives, but could not be
ordered by the prisoner from outside nor could he pay for them out
of his prison earnings if he had chosen to work. None of the unconvicted prisoners in our sample had ever received meals sent in
from outside and our impression from discussion with staff and
prisoners was that the right was comparatively rarely exercised.

THE RIGHT TO REQUEST A SPECIAL CELL PRIVATELY FURNISHED

Prison standing orders appear to make no mention of Rule 25. No accommodation was reserved for such purposes at Winchester, none of
the prisoners in our sample were in possession of private furniture,

bedding or utensils, nor were any relieved of the duty of cleaning
their cells. At no time in our three months' stay at Winchester did
we hear of any unconvicted prisoner who had exercised such rights
either then or in the past.

THE EXCLUSION FROM PRISON REQUIREMENTS CONCERNING HAIRCUTTING

The provision whereby an unconvicted prisoner is exempt from normal
prison haircutting procedures, is not, of course, the definition of
his right to have the haircut, beard or moustache of his choice. It
is designed to protect the evidence of identity - as much in his own
interest as anyone else's - at a subsequent court appearance. As
Standing Order 8(a)16 which was in force at the time of our study
makes clear 'untried prisoners will not be allowed to effect alterations in their personal appearance'. To this end the reception
officer is required to 'take brief particulars of facial appearances' and governors are enjoined to 'take every precaution to
ensure that this order is enforced' and to warn officers 'to be on
their guard against giving prisoners any opportunity of evading it'.
The net effect of this provision was that unconvicted prisoners were
required to shave either in a recess or in their cells with the door
open under the eye of an officer, whereas convicted prisoners could
shave in the privacy of their cells with the doors locked.

THE RIGHT TO CHOOSE WHETHER OR NOT TO WORK

If an untried prisoner elected to work he was employed in No.7 Shop
together with civil prisoners and young prisoners awaiting transfer
to Young Prisoner establishments. The work was not particularly at-
tractive, being mainly mattress assembly, and towards the end of our
fieldwork this workshop was increasingly devoted to the production
of heavy textiles - perhaps more familiarly known as mailbags. Subject to difficulties arising from staff shortages which had
sometimes necessitated its closure, No.7 shop was normally in operation for 5½ hours a day, five days a week. If an untried prisoner
exercised his right not to work, those 5½ hours each day were spent
in his cell - periods quite unrelieved by any other prison activity.
In spite of this rather stark alternative only one of the ten
prisoners in our sample had chosen to work.

THE RIGHT TO UNLIMITED LETTERS AND VISITS

The rights of unconvicted prisoners to send and receive as many
letters as they wished seemed to be fully realised in Winchester.
Certainly we learned of no limitation as to number being imposed on
any individual in our sample. Convicted prisoners were entitled
under the Statutory Rules to one letter each week, and in addition
were permitted at that time to send two 'canteen' letters for which
the prisoners paid the postage. The unconvicted prisoners whom we
interviewed sent out 9.0 letters a month on average compared to 6.6
letters for convicted prisoners. The difference is not statisti-

cally significant however, because of the high degree of variation
in the numbers of letters sent by the small sample of unconvicted
persons. It should be noted that, on average at least, the numbers
of letters sent by untried prisoners were well within the limits
permitted for convicted prisoners. Furthermore there were no
differences in the numbers of letters received - 6.1 per month for
unconvicted and 5.7 for convicted prisoners - which suggests that
there may be little advantage to be gained from the lack of restriction on letters because of the limited circle of persons
available with whom the prisoners, whether convicted or not, can
correspond. The rights of unconvicted prisoners in respect of
letters are 'subject to such conditions as the Secretary of State
may direct' which meant in practice that both incoming and outgoing
mail, though presumably not that involving legal matters under Rule
37 A(1), was censored in the same way as that for sentenced prisoners.

The writing and receiving of letters, however, should be considered in conjunction with the use of visiting facilities. It is
possible that the differences between unconvicted and convicted
prisoners in terms of letters sent and received were lower than
might otherwise have been the case for one, or both, of two reasons.
First, since unconvicted prisoners were permitted visits, without
the need for sending out visiting orders in advance, at 'all reasonable times' except on Sundays when the facilities were fully used by
convicted prisoners, they might have had less need to write letters.
Second, some convicted prisoners may have chosen to write and receive a letter in lieu of a visit which they could do on application
to the governor. Convicted adults, apart from those on appeal to
whom special regulations applied, were entitled to one visit every
eight weeks under the Statutory Rules and young prisoners to one
visit every four weeks. Under some circumstances visits could be
accumulated within certain limits. In practice convicted prisoners
at Winchester were normally permitted one visit each month. In addition both unconvicted and convicted prisoners could receive visits
at the request of officials, and 'welfare' or other 'special' visits
at the discretion of the governor. Unconvicted prisoners in our
sample were visited on average 4.3 times per month; but more than
half the total visits were received by one prisoner who was visited
almost daily and four prisoners out of the ten whom we interviewed
received only one visit or none at all. Convicted prisoners on the
other hand were visited 0.7 times per month. Although trial and
remand prisoners could be visited frequently their visits were
brief, normally lasting only fifteen minutes, and were held in
closed visiting boxes at the main gate. Visits for convicted
prisoners, though less frequent, normally lasted for half an hour
and could normally be held in open visiting rooms in the new reception building. While undoubtedly some unconvicted prisoners did
make full use of the visiting facilities available, many were visited for a total period no greater than the average for convicted men
and in conditions which were a good deal more inhibiting. Civil
prisoners wrote and received letters, and were visited, about as
frequently as convicted prisoners.

THE RIGHT TO HAVE NEWSPAPERS, BOOKS AND OTHER ITEMS SUPPLIED

The right to have books and newspapers sent in from outside is accorded to convicted as well as unconvicted prisoners. The main difference in Winchester seemed to be that convicted prisoners had to exchange their newspapers and periodicals on a one for one basis, and to pass on their books (only paperbacks were allowed) to the prison library after 'a reasonable time' had elapsed, whereas unconvicted prisoners could retain these articles. In fact only two of the ten unconvicted prisoners we spoke to had received any magazine or newspaper from outside prison and only one had any privately provided books in his possession.

Convicted prisoners did not avail themselves of this right very frequently either, but they did have access to the prison library from whose 13,000 volumes they could borrow up to six books at a time; and those prisoners who had successfully applied to dine out had access to prison supplied so-called 'stage' newspapers in B,C and D wings - at least on weekdays. Unconvicted prisoners were not eligible for association, and if they had no newspaper of their own they had no access to any other, whether privately or prison supplied. And although a small supply of books was kept on A wing for their use, they had no access to the main prison library. As a result unconvicted prisoners had more restricted facilities in these respects than many convicted prisoners.

In our interviews we used a check list to assess the number of items which prisoners had in their possession. The check list was not exhaustive and was designed with convicted prisoners in mind. Even so we expected that there would be some differences between convicted and unconvicted prisoners in the numbers of items which had been privately provided or prison supplied. In fact no such differences emerged. After tobacco, both groups spent their earnings or private cash on such items as soap and toothpaste. Only two of our unconvicted sample possessed the writing materials which were permitted under the statutory rules.

It seems from the evidence at Winchester then, that the special provisions for the protection of unconvicted persons in custody, which are valuable but slender enough in theory, mean very little in practice. In fact several reasons conspired to produce a very restrictive regime for these prisoners. First, nearly all the statutory rules were further complicated by supplementary regulations in the standing orders and circular instructions of Prison Department, and some facilities such as special cells, were simply not available at Winchester. Second, although some untried prisoners were able to make extensive use of their rights for unlimited letters and visits, most derived no greater benefit from these provisions than did convicted prisoners from theirs - probably because they knew rather few persons who were able and willing to write or visit. This is not surprising, of course, when one recalls that the most common reason for refusing bail in the first place is because the accused has no fixed abode (Zander, 1971; M.King, 1971). Third, most of the remaining provisions were dependent, directly or indirectly, on the often meagre financial resources of the prisoner or his friends and relations, and his capacity to mobilise them. And finally these very privileges of access to private resources, even though they were rarely used, together with the need to keep different classes of prisoner separate, meant that unconvicted prisoners had little or no access to the prison supplied resources available to convicted prisoners.

In short, while it is not difficult to agree with the late Sir Lionel Fox that the regime for unconvicted prisoners seems 'more depressing' than that for convicted prisoners, the meaning of his assertion that it is none the less a 'less oppressive' one is not altogether clear. Certainly in our wider comparative studies of prison regimes there was a good deal of evidence to suggest that unconvicted prisoners experienced more constraining regimes than convicted prisoners in other prisons, and in several respects at least, more constraining regimes than convicted prisoners within Winchester.

The regime for a prisoner in any prison may be conceived as the outcome of an ongoing negotiation between that prisoner on the one hand, and his fellow prisoners and the staff on the other. The scope for negotiation may vary quite widely from prisoner to prisoner; but though different prisoners may negotiate different outcomes from the same starting point the scope for negotiation is never unlimited. It takes place within a framework of regular routines which are more or less tightly controlled by rules and the available resources. We defined a prison regime therefore, as the application and use of the rules, routines and resources which make up the daily round of life for the prisoner. Thus far in this chapter we have attempted to document the extent to which the unconvicted and civil prisoners in our Winchester sample were able to exercise the main rights accorded them under the Prison Rules. In doing so we have already indicated the ways in which some of the limited prison facilities were distributed among different classes of prisoner; and the ways in which some of the rules and regulations of the establishment were interpreted to apply to particular categories. The measures of prison regimes which we developed, however, were built up from a more detailed consideration of a much wider range of rules, routines and resources as these were applied through the management of important and recurring activities, events and decisions. Our focus was on the routine residential and recreational life of the prisoner. The resulting regime scales provide a convenient and systematic method for comparing many aspects of the regimes experienced by different classes of prisoner not just at Winchester but in other prisons as well. We have provided elsewhere a comparative account of the regimes for convicted prisoners in other prisons (R.D.King, 1972) and in the present chapter we will confine our attention to a necessarily simplified account of the regimes within Winchester. A full discussion of the conceptual basis and statistical properties of the measures is also given elsewhere (R.D.King, 1972) and only a brief outline is required here.

The methods we employed were developed in part from those used by King, Raynes and Tizard (1971) in their assessment of patterns of care in residential institutions. The procedure was as follows. The framework of rules, routines and resources was conceived as constraining or facilitating the activities, choices and relationships of prisoners in several analytically distinct areas of life.

Within each area the regime was conceptualised as a continuous dimension reflecting the degree to which these matters were in fact constrained or facilitated by that framework. For example, one regime dimension, block treatment, was defined as the extent to which the prisoner is required to carry out recurrent activities in the company of other prisoners in a regimented manner. A pool of items was selected during a period of many months of observation and discussion with prisoners and staff in one prison and more limited periods in several others. The items relating to the prisoner activities, choices and relationships under consideration, were allocated to one or another of the regime dimensions as appropriate in the judgment of the research team. Each item was closed ended with a short list of possible responses which could be ranked, e.g.

    Block treatment
    Item 1   Whether or not the prisoner is treated in a regimented
             manner when he goes to 'slop out'.
             0 Prisoner goes individually, at will, to slop out
             1 Prisoner accompanies other inmates at will
             2 Prisoner is filed, marched or paraded to slop out.

Other items in this area were concerned with how prisoners were managed during movement to and from meals, work and so on and the responses were ranked in a similar manner. The items were put into question form in an interview schedule for data collection purposes and a sample of prisoners in four prisons was interviewed. In the analysis ranks were treated as equal intervals and for the purpose of scale construction ranks were used as scores. Following analysis a total of nine scales was standardised on a range of 0 to 99 and each prisoner in the sample was assigned a score on each scale.
    In addition to block treatment four other scales measured different aspects of the routine handling of the activities and relationships of prisoners by the staff: and on each of these scales the higher the score the greater the degree of constraint that is indicated.

    Rigidity was defined as the extent to which the prisoner was required to carry out recurrent activities at fixed times and at fixed intervals. In this area we asked about such matters as the flexibility of times for locking and unlocking and bathing routines and so on.

    Restrictiveness was defined as the extent to which the prisoner was denied access to either places or persons in the prison. Items here included the amount of time for association and whereabouts prisoners took their meals for example. In the event this area produced two scales - restrictiveness within wings and restrictiveness between wings.

    Supervision was defined as the extent to which the prisoner was subject to surveillance during recurrent activities. Items related to the closeness of supervision in the course of movement about the prison, and during leisure time activities like watching television.

A second group of scales measured the degree of autonomy accorded to prisoners in the making of certain kinds of choices. On these scales the higher the scores the greater the degree of autonomy that prisoners enjoyed.

Self-responsibility was defined as the extent to which the prisoner was able to exercise control over his immediate personal activities - how often he could change his shirts, for example, or whether he could control the light in his cell.

Collective responsibility was defined as the extent to which prisoners participated in and exercised control over group activities - such as the organisation of meetings, sports activities and so on.

Finally two further scales measured the degree of social distance between staff and prisoners, and the degree of media isolation which prisoners experienced.

Social distance was defined as the extent to which staff and prisoner worlds were kept separate by social and physical restrictions. Questions related to the numbers of informal contacts between the two groups, the use of space in the wings for staff and inmate purposes and similar matters. High scores indicated high degrees of social distance.

Media isolation was concerned to measure the extent to which each prisoner maintained contact with the outside world via the mass media, and questions were asked about his use of newspapers, magazines, radio and television. High scores indicated high contact with the media and thus a low degree of isolation.

We mentioned earlier that allocation of a prisoner to work meant that he might have a special cell location at Winchester: it also sometimes meant that the prisoner might be locked in it at different times. This was particularly the case for prisoners allocated to special work parties such as the Home Office party which went to the Police College to work, and the parties which served the hospital, the officers' mess, the kitchen and the library. These groups together with certain other individuals were usually in a better position to negotiate some of the conditions under which their sentence was served within the prison and no attempt has been made to delineate these special regimes here. They applied to comparatively few prisoners. At the risk of some over-simplification, however, most of the regime differences in Winchester were to be found between the groups we have already discussed: unconvicted prisoners, civil prisoners, convicted prisoners who did not dine out, and convicted prisoners who did dine out. Table 3.3 displays the mean scale scores and standard deviations on the first five regime scales for each of these groups in our sample at Winchester together with an analysis of variance using the 'F' test. It should be noted that the regime for convicted but unsentenced 'sections' was for all practical purposes identical to that for convicted prisoners who were not eligible for dining out.

TABLE 3.3 Mean regime scale scores, standard deviations and analysis of variance for different classes of prisoner in Winchester

| | | Block treatment | Rigidity | Restrictiveness | | | N |
				Within wing	Between wing	Supervision	
Untried	Mean	80.4	67.0	86.6	73.3	44.3	10
	SD	7.1	13.4	0.0	12.2	6.8	
Civils	Mean	70.1	86.4	86.6	71.5	43.0	5
	SD	30.9	7.6	0.0	15.2	12.8	
Unsentenced and sentenced 'diners-in'	Mean	73.7	79.2	79.1	57.6	56.5	39
	SD	27.9	11.7	14.9	22.5	17.1	
Sentenced 'diners-out'	Mean	60.0	87.9	63.4	55.5	62.0	10
	SD	23.6	11.3	14.6	14.5	19.8	
P less than		.001	.005	.001	NS	NS	64

It can be seen from Table 3.3 that the differences between the means of all these groups on the scales which measure degrees of constraint in the routine handling of prisoners reached statistical significance in the case of block treatment, rigidity and within wing restrictiveness. We were principally concerned, however, to examine differences in regime scores for untried prisoners and the two groups of convicted prisoners, those who dined in cells and those permitted to take meals in association on the landings. And since the inclusion of the extra group of civil prisoners could have influenced the result of the 'F' test we accordingly tested the means for these groups using Sheffé's (1943) approximate 't' test. (Sheffé's test, as supplied in the Statistical Package for the Social Sciences by Nie, Bent and Hull (1970), was preferred here to the conventional 't' test because of the differences in standard deviations of each group.) Whereas the regime for untried prisoners was significantly less rigid and involved significantly less supervision than for either 'diners-in' or 'diners-out' (at the 5 per cent level or better), these unconvicted prisoners were significantly more restricted, both within and between wings than either of the other groups (in all cases at the 1 per cent level). It is worth mentioning, of course, that there is little need to supervise prisoners who for the greater part of the day are locked in cells anyway. In the case of block treatment there was no significant difference between the untried prisoners and the convicted 'diners-in', but 'diners-out' were significantly less regimented (at the 5 per cent level). We should add that in only one of the adult training prisons which were studied in our research programme, and then in only some wings of that prison, did we find higher scores on either the block treatment or the within-wing restrictiveness scales than was the case for untried prisoners in Winchester.

In Table 3.4 we present the mean scores, standard deviations, and an analysis of variance using the 'F' test for all prisoner groups in Winchester on the self-responsibility, collective responsibility, social distance and media isolation scales. No significant differences were found. However, for the reasons cited above, we again tested the mean scores for prisoner groups other than civil prisoners using Sheffé's 't' test. Untried prisoners enjoyed a higher degree of self-responsibility than either 'diners-out' or 'diners-in' (at the 1 per cent level). But there were no significant differences for either collective responsibility or social distance and untried prisoners were actually more isolated from the media (at the 5 per cent level or better) than any other group in the prison. Indeed they were more media-isolated than any adult prisoners in any of the other prisons that we studied - only to be surpassed by their counterparts in the remand centre as we report in chapter 4.

The findings from the application of our regime scales in Winchester then, fill out and confirm the bleak picture which emerged from our analysis of the way in which the statutory rules for special categories of prisoners were interpreted and applied. Unconvicted prisoners, very often men sent to prison in the first place because they have no financial resources or no fixed abode, are held often for weeks or even months, in overcrowded mid-Victorian accommodation. They are locked into their cells for longer periods than any convicted men except those undergoing

TABLE 3.4 Mean regime scale scores, standard deviations and analysis of variance for different classes of prisoner in Winchester

		Self-responsibility	Collective responsibility	Social distance	Media isolation	N
Untried	Mean	35.7	13.0	92.8	25.5	10
	SD	8.3	6.8	8.2	15.1	
Civils	Mean	26.6	11.9	97.1	18.9	5
	SD	8.9	8.3	5.1	15.7	
Unsentenced and sentenced 'diners-in'	Mean	20.4	15.2	92.2	40.1	39
	SD	12.0	6.9	8.3	24.2	
Sentenced 'diners-out'	Mean	17.3	17.5	91.1	47.4	10
	SD	12.7	4.2	9.4	17.1	
P less than		NS	NS	NS	NS	64

punishment, unless they give up their right not to work. Even then they are out of cells only for as long as the least privileged convicted prisoners, and when they are unlocked they are subject to a greater degree of overall constraint than the majority of convicted prisoners who are not under special surveillance for security reasons. Although in principle their conditions may be relieved to some degree by certain privileges in respect of food, letters, visits, newspapers and so on, these are comparatively rarely used, partly because they are out of the financial reach of many un-convicted prisoners. And these privileges are given at the cost of greatly restricted access to facilities which are available to convicted prisoners. Not only do unconvicted prisoners have fewer books to choose from than convicted prisoners, but they have no classes to occupy their time, and no association. They also have the same low degree of responsibility for the events and decisions that make up their daily existence as do convicted prisoners. Civil prisoners occupy a similar position to unconvicted prisoners in some respects and to convicted prisoners in others. Unsentenced prison-ers in the main prison are treated in much the same way as the least privileged persons sentenced to imprisonment. The numbers of prisoners in these categories in our sample are small, but we do not believe, having had three months of fieldwork in which to observe any conflicting evidence, that the picture we have presented can be in any serious way misleading. Moreover there is some reason to believe that Winchester is reasonably typical of local prisons. While the details may vary from place to place and time to time ac-cording to the pressures from the courts, we would be surprised if unconvicted, unsentenced and civil prisoners enjoy very different regimes and conditions elsewhere. To what extent the new remand centres have created regimes more closely geared to the character-istics of their more homogeneous untried and unsentenced population is the question to which we turn in chapter 4.

HM REMAND CENTRE-WINCHESTER

The most surprising thing about remand centres is that their
emergence and existence has received so little comment. With the
exception of a brief description of the location and daily routine
of Risley (Davies, 1970), there is nothing to be read on remand
centres apart from passing acknowledgments in the standard legal and
penological texts that they exist and were authorised by the 1948
Criminal Justice Act. Reasons for this lack of attention are not
hard to find. To some extent it might appear that the need for, and
desirability of, remand centres is self-evident. Remand centres
have reduced the burden that would otherwise have been borne by
local prisons; and perhaps more importantly they have removed most
persons under 21, for this has been their predominant use, from the
experience of prison on remand. Furthermore in campaigning for the
more extensive use of bail, penal reform groups have given maximum
publicity to the generally recognised inadequacies of the local
prisons and have tended to ignore the remand centres with their
largely new and presumably superior material provisions. Finally
there seems to have been an assumption that purpose-built remand
centres would provide a regime appropriate to their task and which
would differentiate them from the multifunctional local prisons.
    Neither Prison Department nor successive governments have done
anything to dispel the belief that remand centres are more suited to
their task than local prisons. The White Paper, 'People in Prison',
ʻin describing the provision of remand centres for persons under 21,
argued that 'only a small proportion of these young men (and women)
will be sentenced to imprisonment, and they ought not to be held in
a prison' (Cmnd 4214, 1969, para.147). This statement glosses over
two issues. First, that many young persons held on remand do not
receive custodial sentences of any kind, not just imprisonment. And
second, that just as large a proportion of adults as young remand
prisoners are released to the community on sentence. Moreover, it
implies not only that the experience of a local prison, given the
present deficiencies of those institutions, might be harmful, but
also that in some sense a remand centre is not a prison. In our
view the differences between remand centres and prisons are more
apparent than real, and we believe that the case for separate institutions to fulfil the remand function has not been established. The

discussion which follows indicates, we think, a need for the public
scrutiny of current remand centre policy.

Provision under the 1948 Act for the creation of remand centres
was even more slowly enacted than was the case with attendance and
detention centres. It was to be thirteen years before the first
remand centre was opened at Ashford in 1961. By 1965 all of the
remand centres now in existence, with the exception of Latchmere
House, had been opened and this completed the programme which had
been planned in the 1950s. The familiar Prison Department problem,
apart from finance, which beset the planners was the difficulty in
finding suitable sites: a difficulty which is reflected in the location of the ten existing centres. The penal philosophy of the
early nineteenth century stressed the priority which was to be attached to the separation of prisoners not only from each other but
also from the pernicious familial and community influences which, it
was argued, had led to the offender's conviction. Many of our isolated training prisons, built for convicts in the nineteenth century, bear witness to this aim. By contrast current penological
thought stresses the desirability of fostering and maintaining the
prisoner's links with the outside world as far as this is consistent
with security. The legacy of the past imposes severe constraints
upon current practice and the difficulties experienced by friends
and relatives when visiting men and women in many of our training
prisons are probably obvious, even if insufficiently documented.
Although for the most part our local prisons are situated close to
the centres of major towns and cities they are not as accessible as
they might be: nearly all of them owe their location to the distribution of population as it was well over a century ago. While the
remand centres are intended to serve contemporary population
centres, their precise locations seem intended more often to mini-
mise the transport problems of the police and the prison service
than those of potential visitors.

Three of the ten remand centres - Cardiff, Exeter and Winchester
are attached to existing local prisons. The remand centre at
Cardiff was in fact converted from one of the wings of the local
prison; the one at Exeter was part purpose-built and part converted
from the old county court offices; and Winchester remand centre was
wholly purpose-built. Five of the remaining centres were built
specially for their present purpose but all seven lie either on the
fringe of, or outside, the urban centres of population which they
predominantly serve. The London area is served by two centres,
Ashford two miles east of Staines, and Latchmere House at Richmond
in Surrey. Brockhill serves the Birmingham area and is situated
three miles from Bromsgrove, some fifteen miles from the centre of
the city. The Durham area is catered for by Low Newton four miles
north of the city and its local prison. Pucklechurch, which serves
the Bristol area, is six miles from the city. Leeds local prison
has its associated remand centre, Thorp Arch, at Boston Spa twelve
miles away. And lastly Risley, which serves Liverpool and
Manchester, is some twelve miles from either.

In his discussion of Risley, Davies (1970) singled out its geographical isolation for special criticism. He argued that visitors
from either Liverpool or Manchester had to travel some twenty-five
miles by road and that since the centre was poorly served by public

transport those people without access to a car incurred a journey of anything from two to four hours and costs, at that time, of between ten and fifteen shillings. We do not know the extent to which the other remand centres suffer from these difficulties because no work appears to have been done on the matter. But it is clear that remand centres typically have larger catchment areas than the local prisons with which they are administratively associated, and even where the centres are reasonably close to the main conurbations it is unlikely that the majority of families who might wish to visit will live in the immediate urban area. In the case of centres for women and girls, of course, the catchment areas are very large indeed - four institutions at Low Newton, Pucklechurch, Risley and Holloway serve the needs of the whole of England and Wales. In these circumstances the distance between the institutions and the main public transport routes and interchanges is a major, perhaps crucial, consideration. Unfortunately, the extra remand accommodation which is planned is not going to meet this requirement any better than the existing facilities. Further building is to take place at Pucklechurch, Low Newton and Thorp Arch, and of the five proposed new centres only one, at Norwich, is to be adjacent to a local prison and easily accessible from a city centre (Cmnd 5375, 1973, Appendix 2).

This is not a case of the Prison Department exhibiting a callous disregard for the convenience of remand prisoners and their families. In the short term, Prison Department has no choice but to accept anyone whom the courts decide to deprive of his liberty - although in our view it could do much more to advertise the failings of the system which might deter the courts from some of their actions. Be that as it may, in recent years the courts have refused bail to a rapidly growing number of persons under 21 years so that the pressures on the Department to build new accommodation have been great. Moreover, city centre sites, which would avoid the criticisms offered above, would not only be difficult to find but would be extremely expensive were they available. Even so it is hard to see how Prison Department can feel that the existing and planned centres go very far towards meeting one of the declared objectives of remand centres - 'to provide the facilities, including those for visiting by solicitors, probation officers and relatives, to which an unsentenced person is entitled' (Cmnd 4214, 1969, para.147). In principle, there seems no reason why the same objective would not have been better met by providing extra and better visiting accommodation in the local prisons.

'People in Prison' cites two other central purposes of the remand centres: 'to detain in suitable and secure conditions those remanded in custody' and 'to provide a service to the courts by the assessment of those unsentenced persons by experienced staff, including medical staff' (Cmnd 4214, 1969, para.147). Again the same purposes are served, or striven for, by the local prisons. It is true that under section 48 of the Criminal Justice Act 1948 the Secretary of State was obliged to provide in remand centres 'facilities for enquiries into medical and mental health to assist the court in determining the most suitable way of dealing with his case' - and that this obligation was re-affirmed under section 43 of the Prison Act 1952. But in practice there is no less an expectation that the same service shall be provided by the local prisons, and to the extent that they have facilities for the medical examination and treatment discussed elsewhere in the White Paper (para. 165), they do provide it. In fact we have not been able to find, either in the White Paper or elsewhere, any statement of policy about the operation of remand centres that would demand any serious difference in regime between them on the one hand and local prisons on the other. The Home Office, in its memorandum of evidence to the abortive Royal Commission on the Penal System, limited itself to a virtual re-statement of its statutory obligations. And in 'People in Prison' no opportunity was taken even to suggest that special attention could be paid to the statutory rights of unconvicted offenders in remand centres which could not be achieved elsewhere.

Fox's view of the remand centre would have required some real departures from the local prison model although it is by no means clear that these would have worked to the advantage of unconvicted and unsentenced prisoners either in terms of their daily routine or the protection of their statutory rights. His remarks were as notable, however, for their brevity as for their Utopian ambition; 'if these centres are to do the work required of them they will be not only places of safe custody but laboratories of research into the causes and treatment of juvenile delinquency, with large and specialised staffs of medical, psychological and social workers' (Fox, 1952, p.341). Leaving aside what now seems a quaintly naive and positivistic undertone, Fox does not indicate how these aims are to be achieved in daily practice especially with a population whose stay in the institution ought, at least, to be so short-lived. The Home Office memorandum was more realistic, and pointed to the difficulties of doing anything with such a short-stay population, though it expressed the hope that 'an inmate might be no worse for his stay should he be found not guilty or should he receive a non-custodial sentence, but may have benefited by his detention in the centre' (HMSO, 1967, vol.1, pp. 8-9). One may well wonder just how a person found not guilty could possibly have benefited from his detention, but once again it should be noted that no indication is given as to how remand centres are supposed to succeed in these matters where, by implication, the local prisons have failed.

The key to the lack of real distinction between the remand centres and the prisons is to be found in the evidence submitted to the Royal Commission by the Magistrates' Association, who lamented the fact that remand centres were 'still under Prison Rules and not in accordance with the Criminal Justice Act 1948' (HMSO, 1967, vol. 2, para.64, p.17). It would seem that this reference is to the presumed spirit rather than to the letter of the 1948 Act for s.48.6 merely states that 'the Prison Acts, 1865 to 1898 shall, subject to such adaptations and modifications as may be made by rules of the Secretary of State, apply to remand centres, detention centres and borstals, and to persons detained therein, as they apply to prisons and prisoners.' However there is some reason to suppose that real differences between the rules for these institutions were intended because s.47 of the Prison Act 1952 empowered the Secretary of State to make rules for 'prisons, remand centres, detention centres and borstal institutions respectively'. And in view of the fact that separate rules were subsequently introduced by statutory instruments for detention centres (SI no.1432, 1952), attendance centres (SI no. 1990, 1958), borstals (SI no.387, 1964) and prisons (SI no.388, 1964), the complaint of the Magistrates' Association in respect of remand centres does seem justified. Today, as at the time the Magistrates' Association made the complaint, remand centres and remand centre prisoners are governed by the 1964 Prison Rules and those rules do not distinguish between a prison and a remand centre. If regimes are determined solely by statutory rules then we should not expect remand centres to differ from remand wings in local prisons.

Given that most remand centre prisoners are under 21 years of age, we should perhaps expect there to be special administrative provisions which apply to this age group, and thus effectively set remand centres apart from adult institutions at least. Indeed there are some such provisions, deriving not from the Prison Rules - which do not differentiate young from adult prisoners - but from the Prison Department's standing orders. But they do not amount to much, especially in so far as they relate to unconvicted and un- sentenced young prisoners. The basic rule that unconvicted prison- ers 'shall be kept out of contact with convicted prisoners as far as this can reasonably be done' (SI no.388, 1964, Rule 3) is elaborated in Standing Order 8(a) - 22(3) whereby 'untried prisoners under 21 years of age will be segregated from adult prisoners and, so far as is practicable, those who have not previously been in prison or borstal will be separated from others.' The same standing order goes on to say that untried prisoners under 21 years of age 'will be encouraged to work and to take part in physical training and edu- cational and other activities arranged for convicted young prison- ers. In so far as they must associate with convicted young prison- ers for these purposes, separation, as far as is practicable, must be maintained.' But in fact the single provision which is likely to distinguish young from adult prisoners refers to physical exercise and is incorporated in Standing Order 7(c)-7 which states that 'young prisoners will receive no less than two sessions of physical education each week and they shall be regarded as part of the normal working day.'

In summary then, the rules governing remand centres are no different from those applying to prisons: as far as both the statu- tory rules and standing orders are concerned, remand centres are prisons. Furthermore, the statutory provisions distinguishing un- convicted from convicted prisoners which we reviewed in chapter 3 apply to all prisoners whatever their age. The only important vari- ation likely to be found is that all prisoners under 21 years - un- tried, unsentenced and sentenced and whether housed in remand centres or local prisons - receive more physical exercise than is normally the case for adults. From this review, therefore, we must conclude that if remand centres are really different from remand wings in local prisons, and there has clearly been a widespread though vague expectation that they ought to be, then these differ- ences can only be discovered from a detailed inspection of their day-to-day running. For whatever may have been done through in- formal planning or exhortation the successive Secretaries of State and the Prison Department have not seen fit to give any statutory or bureaucratic foundation to any differentiation that may have emerged.

During the course of our fieldwork at Winchester we were also
able to examine the regime in HM remand centre. Because our main
concern was with the comparison of regimes for adult prisoners
the amount of time and resources that we were able to devote to
the remand centre was very much less than we would have wished.
As a result we are aware that in this discussion of Winchester
remand centre our remarks are based on data collected from very
small numbers indeed. Nevertheless it was clear from the consistency of our results with our general observations, and with
the informal comments of both detainees and staff, that the findings
reported here reasonably represented the regime at the centre in
1971.

Winchester remand centre was officially opened on 21 July 1964.
The centre was purpose-built and occupies an area outside the
Winchester prison complex but adjacent to it. The two institutions
are about half-a-mile from the city centre and court house. On one
side the remand centre shares the brick perimeter wall of the main
prison. On the other three sides it is bordered by a 17 ft high
chain link security fence topped by coiled barbed wire. The remand
centre compound can be entered both from the main prison and through
its own external gatehouse. It is kept under surveillance by the
same dog patrols that provide additional perimeter security for the
main prison.

The buildings comprise essentially one three-storey rectangular
block or main building to which two accommodation wings are attached
at right angles. The area between the wings is used as the main
exercise square. The two wings are almost identical in design and
lay-out; in each are two floors with ten cells per floor arranged
five on each side of a central corridor. Toilet, washing and
showering facilities are provided on each floor at the end of the
corridor. Each cell is 8 ft by 7 ft and contains a small square
table, a single upright chair and two bunk beds so that the accommodation is cramped by any standards. As one of the measures taken to
accord with Rule 3 one wing, known as 'Temple', accommodates untried
prisoners and the other, 'Wykeham', houses convicted, both sentenced
and unsentenced, prisoners. These accommodation wings provide 78
beds in all, an office having taken the place of a cell on one
landing.

Because of the sloping nature of the site the reception area is
effectively situated on the first floor of the main building. The
ground floor contains the kitchen, stores, staff offices, dining and
association rooms and, in separate sections, the observation and
punishment areas. Alongside the reception area on the first floor
is a large room and several cubicles in which open, closed and
special visits may be received. The second floor contains rooms
used variously as workshops, classrooms, stores, offices and the
hospital. The diagnostic and assessment function of the remand
centre is reflected in the extent and variety of the accommodation
originally provided in 1964 for a maximum of 39 prisoners. On the
ground floor, close to the staff offices, are a number of rooms
which were intended for prisoners requiring special observation.
Today these rooms are routinely used as dormitories for persons immediately after reception and prior to discharge or simply to cater
for an overflow from the accommodation wings. In 1971 those obser-

vation rooms, or 'grade rooms' as they are known in Winchester, provided 30 beds: together with the two punishment cells, the ten beds
in the hospital dormitory and the 78 beds which made up the certified accommodation in the wings, the total number of beds which
could be brought into use, if necessary, was 120. Table 4.1 indicates that in 1972, on some occasions at least, almost all of those
beds were needed.

The increase in certified accommodation at Winchester is similar
in magnitude to that which the Prison Department reported for other
remand centres and which we discussed in chapter 2. In Winchester
the increase in capacity was achieved not by additional building but
through the redesignation, for normal accommodation, of rooms which
were originally intended for other purposes. As a result in 1972,
when the average population was more than twice that for which the
centre was built only eight years earlier, Winchester remand centre
was officially said to be only 8 per cent over-occupied (Cmnd 5375,
1973, Appendix 3). Even so the reallocation of space did not keep
pace with the demand for beds, for at times in 1972 the population
approached three times the original capacity. Table 4.1 reports the
changes in certified accommodation, the average daily population and
the greatest number of persons held, for each year since the centre
opened.

TABLE 4.1 Winchester remand centre - certified accommodation and
average daily population

	1965	1966	1967	1968	1969	1970	1971	1972
Certified accommodation	43	43	43	43	43	43	64	78
Average daily population	41	43	47	44	53	71	81	84
Average usage	95.4	100.0	109.3	102.3	123.3	165.1	126.6	107.7
Greatest number of inmates	60	54	63	56	68	104	113	115

Note: No separate figures on population in the remand centres were
published by Prison Department for 1964, the year in which
Winchester remand centre was opened.

Average daily population figures, of course, smooth out the peaks
and troughs in the demand for places. Compared with training
prisons the population of all establishments with a remand function
is subject to wide weekly and even daily fluctuation. In consequence local prisons and remand centres have to be organised as much
to meet the worst contingencies as to meet the average situation.
It can be seen from Table 4.1 that the greatest number of persons

housed each year at Winchester remand centre was very much larger
than the certified accommodation, and that this excess increased
substantially after 1969. Thus during our fieldwork in 1971, when
the certified accommodation was 64 and the average population around
80 prisoners, the centre was organised to accommodate up to 108
persons excluding the permanent beds in the punishment and hospital
areas. This was accomplished by refurnishing all the original cells
built for one prisoner so that they could accommodate two. Even so
by the end of that year the centre had sometimes housed as many as
113 prisoners. In order to have done so the centre must have used
either hospital or punishment accommodation for boys who would
normally have been housed elsewhere.

It is important to note, therefore, that overcrowding does not
just end with the cramped conditions in the cells. It also involves
the loss of accommodation that could be used for educational, recreational or industrial purposes - and which might have been thought
more necessary when the population is 'doubled-up' than when it was
originally provided. Moreover such accommodation may be effectively
lost even though the institution is not 'full', for an institution
which has to plan for occasional excessive over-use is always likely
to keep some accommodation in readiness for any possible influx of
receptions.

Some variations in regimes at different remand centres seem
likely to have developed over the years for as we mentioned earlier
some centres were purpose-built, some are attached to local prisons,
some cater for women and girls, and some are more isolated than
others. But since all remand centres suffer much the same pressures
on staff and resources, the scope for variation can hardly be great.
It is probable therefore that the regime which we describe for
Winchester remand centre is typical of remand centres generally - or
at least of those accommodating men and boys. At Winchester remand
centre we interviewed staff about the daily routine of the establishment and then spoke to a sample of prisoners about the regime
as it affected them. Our sample consisted of twelve prisoners who
were the occupants of randomly selected bed spaces in the two
accommodation wings. In our interviews we used the same schedules
which we and our colleagues had devised for use in adult prisons.
The responses were checked as far as this was possible against our
own observations. In this way a comprehensive account of the
regimes for these prisoners was developed which could be compared
directly with the regimes experienced by adult prisoners on remand
in Winchester prison and by the sentenced prisoners whom we interviewed both in Winchester and elsewhere.

We can begin our discussion of the regime in the remand centre,
as we did for the main prison, with a consideration of the extent to
which Rule 3(2) - that unconvicted prisoners 'shall be kept out of
contact with convicted prisoners as far as this can reasonably be
done' - was satisfied. Though the remand centre had two entrances,
each new reception, convicted or unconvicted, usually entered the
compound through the centre's own vehicle gate. He may well have
shared the vehicle which brought him from the court, however, with
adult prisoners destined for the main prison. And it was not
unusual for a prisoner on subsequent occasions to leave for, and
return from, the court via the door to the main prison. On these

occasions both adult and young prisoners, convicted and unconvicted, shared escort officers and transport as well as accommodation and eating facilities at the court. All prisoners entering the remand centre were received in the reception area on the first floor of the main building. The reception process was much the same as that found in any local prison with perhaps one exception: during the waiting period when property, clothing and personal details were checked and recorded there was no separation between the unconvicted, the unsentenced and the sentenced. But by the evening the unconvicted were differentiated from the convicted, each spending their first night in separate 'grade' rooms. On the following day the new prisoner returned to the reception area. There he was medically examined, interviewed by the chaplain, and sent before a reception board chaired either by an assistant governor or, more probably, by a principal officer. If he applied to do so, he could be interviewed by a welfare officer from the main prison. The reception board checked the prisoner's property, warrant and documentation, outlined his legal rights, and allocated him to a cell in Temple wing if he was yet to be tried and in Wykeham if he was already convicted.

Whether housed in Temple or Wykeham all prisoners experienced the same basic daily routine. Although during our fieldwork the regime was somewhat affected by rewiring and redecorating operations, we were still able to discover the 'normal' daily routine from our respondents, and we were able to check the validity of our data on subsequent visits to the centre during more 'normal' times. It was as follows:

Time	Activity
07.00-07.15	Staff come on duty.
07.15-07.50	Unlocked for breakfast in dining room.
07.50-08.50	In cells, staff at breakfast.
08.50-09.30	Unlocked for washing, shaving and slopping out on landing.
09.30-11.00	Some prisoners given work or taken to gymnasium (if staff or work available), remainder locked in cells.
11.00-11.30	Exercise in remand centre exercise area.
11.30-11.45	Locked in cells.
11.45-12.15	Unlocked for lunch in dining room.
12.15-13.45	Locked in cells, staff at lunch.
13.45-14.15	Exercise in remand centre exercise area.
14.15-15.45	Work for some (if available), remainder locked in cells.
15.45-16.45	Locked in cells, staff at tea.
16.45-17.15	Unlocked for tea in dining room.
17.15-18.00	Locked in cells.
18.00-19.50	Some unlocked for classes, remainder locked up until 18.20 when association begins.
19.50-07.15	Locked in cells. Supper served in cells at 20.15.

If work, exercise, evening classes and association were fully provided in accordance with this official routine then a prisoner in Winchester remand centre would spend almost 16 hours a day locked in his cell. But in a situation where staff time was largely taken up by reception and escort duties, and where space for association, classes and work was severely restricted, the constraints imposed by Rule 3(2) often meant, in effect, that the unconvicted could be out of their cells only at the expense of the convicted being confined to theirs - and vice versa. As a result many activities were a- vailable to each group of prisoners only on alternate mornings, afternoons or evenings. The mean time spent in cells on the last weekday preceding interview, for both convicted and unconvicted re- spondents in our sample, was a little over 17 hours. In this re- spect, therefore, the unconvicted prisoners were some 4 hours a day better off than their counterparts in the main prison while the convicted prisoners were 2 hours worse off. Three prisoners, who had special responsibilities for serving and clearing up after meals spent only about 14 hours in cells: but some of the remainder who had either not been able to work or whose turn it was to miss as- sociation in the evening, spent more than 19 hours in cellular con- finement. At weekends the routine was different. The mid-morning periods were taken up by general cleaning, exercise and voluntary church attendance. Although some prisoners could watch television for part of the afternoon there was no evening association and all meals were taken in cells. Thus on Saturdays and Sundays all prisoners were locked up from 4 p.m. until 7 a.m. Indeed the of- ficial routine involved at least 18 hours a day of confinement in cells. Eight of our twelve respondents reported that they had been confined to their cells for between 18 and 20 hours on the Saturday and Sunday prior to their interview. The remainder had spent only 14 or 15 hours in cells because they had to perform kitchen or other special duties.

Work, or rather its absence, had been a cause for concern for many years to the successive assistant governors in charge of the remand centre. No special provision was made when the centre was built, because it was then thought that prisoners would be usefully employed on cleaning and maintenance duties. In 1965 an officer in- structor was allocated to the remand centre and work involving the simple assembly of a small plastic aerosol component was found. But without a workshop it was difficult to supervise this task in the two or three offices which had been converted to house the un- convicted and the convicted in separate rooms. In any case the in- structor was often needed to relieve colleagues in the main prison, and the supply of work was intermittent. Many staff took the view that the work was too boring and sedentary for the young and ener- getic prisoners with whom they had to deal. It often happened while we were in Winchester that prisoners were either left locked up for work periods, or that they worked in small groups for as little as half-an-hour at a time before being returned to their cells. There is, of course, no easy solution to this problem. Remand centre prisoners are in custody for too short a period to learn work which might be more interesting, and in Winchester there is no room in which less sedentary work could be carried out even if it could be found. However, it still has to be said that little is done to al- leviate the extreme boredom which prisoners reported when locked in their cells during 'work time'.

The original design of the remand centre provided only one dining room. When there were only thirty to forty prisoners in the centre this room was sufficient to house both convicted and unconvicted prisoners at separate tables. But as the population grew the room could no longer contain the numbers involved and the separation arrangements became progressively strained. In 1971 the chapel, which was next to the dining room, was converted into a second room for association and dining purposes to enable all prisoners to take their meals at a single sitting with convicted and unconvicted prisoners now in separate rooms.

Some attempts at separation were purely symbolic. Thus all prisoners in the remand centre took their exercise at the same time, and separation was achieved by making the unconvicted and the convicted walk around the yard in separate caterpillars a few feet apart.

In spite of the precautions taken to keep convicted and unconvicted prisoners apart complete separation was no more possible in the remand centre than it had been in the main prison. In addition to the possibility of contact between different classes of prisoner on escort, at reception and during exercise there were further opportunities when meals were served and cleared away, and when prisoners were waiting for visits or to see the doctor or other staff. However it is worth pointing out that, to the extent that the separation rule is justified by the need to avoid contamination of the possibly innocent by the criminally sophisticated, then separation was less necessary in the remand centre than the main prison. In the main prison the unconvicted had to be protected from the large body of convicted and sentenced prisoners, many of whom were serious recidivists. In the remand centre sentenced prisoners were rare. For the most part unconvicted persons had to be protected from their convicted and as yet unsentenced fellows many of whom would be deemed sufficiently unversed in crime to merit a non-custodial disposal. It is true that there could be occasional contact with adult prisoners: on escorts to and from the courts, when remand centre prisoners visited the gymnasium in the main prison, and when parties from the prison came to work in the centre. But such contacts were typically very brief. Of course, to the extent that the separation rule is justified by the presumption of innocence, then the failure to separate the unconvicted from the convicted continues to give cause for concern. In any case sufficient time is spent in close confinement for the other Statutory Rules to be important sources for protection to the unconvicted, and it is to a consideration of these that we now turn.

RULE 17(4) THE RIGHT TO HAVE PRIVATE MEDICAL ATTENTION

As with our sample of unconvicted prisoners in the main prison none of our respondents in the remand centre had had the benefit of private medical services and neither did we hear of anyone who had done so. Further, none of our respondents had attempted to obtain the services of his own doctor and none appeared to know that such a course of action was open to him. (Prison Department states that it is their aim to advise all unconvicted prisoners of their rights, as evidenced by the publication of Information Card 135M - Notes for Guidance of Unconvicted Prisoners, which should be 'readily available in the remand centre'. While this card may have been available on request, it was not shown to us nor did we see it displayed either in cells or elsewhere in Winchester remand centre.)

RULE 20(1) THE RIGHT TO WEAR OWN CLOTHES

In the main prison we found that half of our unconvicted respondents were dressed partly or entirely in their own clothes: the remainder wore 'browns' either on, or some time after, reception because of the limited supply of personal clothing available to them. In the remand centre not only did all six of the unconvicted prisoners interviewed wear 'browns' but during the three months that we were in the centre no prisoner was ever seen dressed in any item of personal clothing. The prisoners in our sample said that they had been instructed on reception to hand in their own clothes and had been issued with full prison kit, as a matter of course. None of our respondents was aware that there was any possibility of retaining his own clothing.

RULE 21(1) THE RIGHT TO HAVE FOOD SENT IN

The right to have food sent in is circumscribed by standing order interpretations as we noted in chapter 3. None of the prisoners interviewed in the main prison had exercised this right and none had done so in the remand centre. In the main prison it was our impression that anyone receiving food or drink from outside would provoke considerable comment: in the remand centre the event appeared unheard of.

RULE 25 THE RIGHT TO REQUEST A SPECIAL CELL PRIVATELY FURNISHED

As in the main prison, none of the prisoners in our sample were in possession of private furnishings of any description nor had anyone made arrangements to have his cell cleaned for him. Since no accommodation was set aside for the purpose it is difficult to see how this provision could have been exercised.

RULE 26(2) THE EXCLUSION FROM PRISON REQUIREMENTS CONCERNING HAIRCUTTING

As we noted in chapter 3, this rule is double-edged. It is less a right than an attempt to ensure that the accused does not alter his appearance. It may protect the unconvicted prisoner against an enforced 'short-back-and-sides' but it also prevents him from adopting such a style whilst he is untried and in custody. There was no difference, nor could there have been, between the main prison and the remand centre regarding this rule.

RULE 28(5) THE RIGHT TO CHOOSE WHETHER OR NOT TO WORK

Although the right to refuse work meant spending work periods locked in cells, only one of the ten unconvicted prisoners interviewed in the main prison had opted to work and was in fact working. In the remand centre all of the unconvicted prisoners interviewed were working albeit intermittently and often for very short periods. The unconvicted prisoners in the remand centre said that they were simply assigned to assembly work with the officer instructor or to those maintenance and service tasks required by staff for the smooth running of the centre. At no time did we hear of an unconvicted prisoner being permitted to remain in his cell because he had chosen not to work nor did we hear of any prisoner expressing a wish not to work. Whether this was because of a preference for work or ignorance of rights we do not know. But it is important to note that it was time spent at work which largely accounted for the longer period out of cells enjoyed by unconvicted prisoners in the remand centre when compared to their adult counterparts in the main prison.

RULE 34(1) THE RIGHT TO UNLIMITED LETTERS AND VISITS

No unconvicted prisoner in the remand centre reported any restriction on his right either to send or receive letters. However, as we note in our discussion of the main prison the circumstances surrounding a remand in custody are such that it is unlikely that the number of letters an unconvicted prisoner may wish to send, or can hope to receive, will exceed the letter allowance of a convicted prisoner. The average number of letters sent out by our sample of unconvicted prisoners was 5.25 per month (since some prisoners had been in custody for only two or three weeks figures were standardised for one month) and the number received was 2.25. Our sample of convicted prisoners in the remand centre both received and sent 2.3 letters per month. Many of the convicted but unsentenced prisoners had previously been held in custody as untried prisoners for the same offence, and were thus effectively at a later stage of their period of incarceration. It may be the case that the greater number of letters sent out by unconvicted prisoners reflects this career development, with several letters being sent out soon after reception to inform friends and relatives of their whereabouts. Many of these letters seem to go unanswered, but it may be that some of them lead to visits which are not taken up until the prisoner has reached the next stage of his career as a convicted prisoner. Certainly the convicted prisoners in our sample received 2.3 visits per month compared to only 1.5 visits for the unconvicted prisoners. All prisoners in our sample in the remand centre sent and received fewer letters than the adults in the main prison. We are unable to say why this should have been so. But if it should have been through difficulties of written communication the remand centre did nothing to compensate prisoners through more generous visiting arrangements: most visits lasted only fifteen minutes and the longest we recorded was half an hour.

RULE 41(1) THE RIGHT TO HAVE NEWSPAPERS, BOOKS AND OTHER ITEMS SUPPLIED

In the main prison we found that very few unconvicted prisoners were in receipt of any newspapers, magazines or books from outside and that no difference was found between convicted and unconvicted prisoners regarding private possessions. In the remand centre private provision was rarer still. Only one unconvicted prisoner was receiving a private newspaper and none had received a magazine or a book. Indeed the overall picture in the remand centre was a depressing one. Although five daily and three Sunday newspapers were delivered to the remand centre, unconvicted and unsentenced prisoners were not entitled to read them. No unconvicted and only one convicted prisoner reported having seen a prison-supplied newspaper on the day prior to interview and most said that there were no newspapers available. We were told by some, however, that newspapers were sometimes to be found in classrooms in support of current affairs discussions. The remand centre had no library. Staff maintained that vandalism in the centre was so bad that it was not worth providing books in good condition. Accordingly the remand centre received discarded books from the main prison - a sorry collection of battered volumes which were distributed amongst the cells. All prisoners reported having found five or six such books in their cell on arrival. Most still possessed the same volumes which they had read during their period of custody.

Both convicted and unconvicted prisoners received 22½p per week regardless of the amount of work they had done. This could be spent in the canteen and was typically used to buy tobacco and such luxuries as soap, shampoo and toothpaste. Unconvicted prisoners could only spend up to 75p each week from private cash, (a measure introduced, we were told, to prevent bartering) even though no limits were imposed by Prison Standing Orders. All of the prisoners interviewed were asked to go through a check-list of items that they might have in their possession; in each case the tally was a bleak one. There was little evidence to support the contention of overspending however that might be defined, nor was there any indication that any prisoner in our sample had the resources to be extravagant with or without the limits imposed by staff.

From this survey of the statutory rights of unconvicted prisoners it is clear that they gained no significant advantage over their adult neighbours from being detained in the remand centre rather than the prison. If Winchester is a fair reflection of what happens elsewhere, and there is some reason to think that it may be, then it is not surprising that the White Paper 'People in Prison' made no mention of the better protection of the rights of the unconvicted in the remand centres.

The evidence derived from the application of our measures of prison regimes, which we discussed in chapter 3, only serves to reinforce the impressions of the remand centre gained in other ways. Table 4.2 presents the regime scale scores for the untried prisoners in Temple wing and the convicted prisoners, including sentenced prisoners, in Wykeham wing. There were no civil prisoners in the remand centre at the time of our study.

TABLE 4.2 Mean regime scale scores, standard deviations and analysis of variance for different classes of prisoner in Winchester remand centre

| | | Block treatment | Rigidity | Restrictiveness | | | | | | | N |
				Within wing	Between wing	Super-vision	Self resp.	Coll. resp.	Soc. dist.	Media isol.	
Temple wing (untried)	Mean	86.4	84.1	57.9	96.7	63.2	10.1	0.0	89.4	0.0	4
	SD	4.7	18.5	0.0	6.4	10.4	4.2	0.0	4.1	0.0	
Wykeham wing (unsentenced and sentenced)	Mean	74.7	90.8	55.0	88.7	55.3	23.0	7.6	92.5	3.7	8
	SD	31.2	13.7	3.1	12.7	19.7	12.5	8.5	5.2	10.5	
P less than		NS	NS	NS	NS	NS	0.01	NS	NS	NS	12

It can be seen from Table 4.2 that the regimes for the untried
prisoners and convicted prisoners in the remand centre, at least as
measured by these scales, were virtually identical. Only in the case
of the self-responsibility scale was a statistically significant
difference found between the mean scores for the two groups: and
here the difference was in favour of convicted prisoners. The
difference is largely accounted for by the fact that convicted
prisoners, who had typically been in the centre for longer than the
unconvicted prisoners, were more likely to be given jobs which required them, or enabled them, to exercise a limited degree of choice
and responsibility. The similarity in the other regime scale scores
for the two wings, of course, reflects the fact that the authorities
themselves did not differentiate between them. Indeed most activities - meals, work, recreation and so on - were arranged for the
centre as a whole and not for the separate wings which merely shared
the available facilities as equitably as possible.

The general pattern of regime scale scores for both groups in the
remand centre was remarkably similar to that we reported for untried
prisoners in the main prison in chapter 3: namely a high degree of
constraint on the block treatment, rigidity, restrictiveness and
supervision scales, and a low degree of autonomy on the self- and
collective responsibility scales. Indeed the levels of constraint
were generally higher, and the levels of autonomy generally lower, in
the remand centre than in the main prison. About the same levels of
social distance between staff and prisoners were found in both institutions, but both groups of prisoners in the remand centre were by
far the most media-isolated of any prisoners in any establishment
that we have studied.

It is true, of course, that prisoners in Winchester remand centre
found life somewhat more comfortable, warmer, less noisy and sweeter
smelling than they would have had they been housed in the nineteenth-
century prison next door. Such differences counted for a great deal
and should not lightly be dismissed - although it is fair to say that
the cells in which remand centre prisoners spent most of their time
were smaller than was thought necessary more than a hundred years
ago. But if any attempt had been made to provide a more relaxed, or
in any way different, regime in the remand centre from that to be
found in the main prison, we were unable to find any evidence to show
that the effort had been successful.

We have already noted that all remand centres are governed by the
Prison Rules and thus are not to be differentiated from the prisons
at this level. But in Winchester, at least, there were additional
organisational reasons which would have made it difficult to provide
a radically different regime in the remand centre even if one were
wanted. Winchester prison and Winchester remand centre were in fact
organisationally inter-dependent institutions, with ultimate responsibility for the management of both falling to the governor of
HM Prison, Winchester. Day-to-day responsibility was delegated to an
assistant governor, but he also had routine duties in the main prison
in addition to his occasional deputisation for the governor or deputy
governor. The custodial staff in the centre were more or less perma-
nently seconded from the main prison. Their position was analogous
to the 'fixed' posts in most prisons whereby staff are allocated to
posts such as gate officer or library officer for a specified period

to ensure continuity. At the time of our study the remand centre
staff included one principal officer and two senior officers with
about a dozen basic grade officers. None of the remand centre staff,
however, was entirely beyond the reach of the 'detail office' which
decided on the allocation of staff to duties in the main prison. As
a result remand centre officers were frequently called upon to do
overtime duties either as escorts, or in the main prison itself, as
occasion demanded.

The two institutions shared other specialist staff also. Physical
education instructors from the main prison supervised exercise in the
remand centre, and for some recreational activities groups of boys
were regularly brought over to the prison gymnasium to use the facilities there. The moral and spiritual welfare of the boys in the
remand centre was the concern of the chaplain and Church Army captain
from the prison. One of the four welfare officers then in post at
the prison specialised in attending to the needs of the remand centre
prisoners, but his duties were not confined to the centre, and he was
quite unable to deal with every case that might have made demands on
his time. Doctors and hospital officers made visits from the prison
hospital to attend reception boards and to make periodic ward rounds
for prisoners housed in the sick bay. Boys requiring more continuous
observation, or attention from a doctor, either because of sickness
or because of a court request for a report, were transferred to the
more fully equipped and staffed hospital in the main prison.

In spite of the proposed diagnostic and court reporting functions
of remand centres, a separate medical facility hardly existed at
Winchester. The hospital bay at the centre never had a permanent
establishment of hospital officers, and space set aside for observation purposes had been progressively taken over for other uses.
Moreover we could find no evidence that custodial staff had been
specially selected or trained for their work. The officers we spoke
to did not think they had been chosen for their posts because of any
particular interest they had expressed, or of training or experience
they had received. Analysis of the material we collected on the age,
training and experience of these officers showed them to be in no way
distinguishable from their colleagues in the main prison. There was
no in-service training programme for remand centre officers, and none
was planned for the future. No one to whom we spoke in either institution suggested that a staff training scheme was necessary, or that
a different kind of job specification would have been appropriate for
the remand centre staff. Since the organisational structure for the
two establishments was virtually identical it is not hard to see why.

Perhaps the recommendations of the Streatfeild Report (Cmnd 1289,
1961) about making reports to the courts realistically reflect the
lack of trained staff and the pressure on resources. Certainly the
guidance given to governors in the Standing Orders about these
matters falls far short of what might have been expected had Fox's
'laboratories of research' come to fruition. The standing orders
state that:

Except where the court otherwise directs, reports should be prepared before the hearing on those offenders only who are:
  i) committed for trial on indictment; or
  ii) committed for a borstal sentence under Section 28 of the
      Magistrates' Courts Act 1952, as amended by the Criminal
      Justice Act, 1961; or

iii)   committed for sentence under Section 29 of the Magistrates'
       Courts Act 1952;
and who are:
defendants eligible for borstal training who have previously
served a custodial sentence of imprisonment, borstal training or
detention centre, or about whom the governor has information a-
vailable which would assist the court.
And with reference to pre-trial reports the Orders state that the
'governor will submit reports only in cases where there is available
to him some record of the defendant's performance during a previous
custodial sentence' and that he is 'not required to provide ... an
assessment of the defendant's suitability for borstal training'.
Indeed elsewhere the Orders assert that such reports 'will be a
factual statement of information and will not include any expression
of opinion except where the court has asked for this to be done'. It
is hardly surprising therefore, that in Winchester remand centre at
least, the preparation of court reports constituted a routine bureaucratic duty which could be fulfilled without any restructuring of
roles for custodial staff. Anything resembling diagnostic activity -
as when the court requested specialist information before sentence -
was undertaken by outsiders, the doctors or welfare officer from the
main prison and by visiting probation officers.
    In sum, remand centres were introduced with two key objectives in
mind over and above the holding of persons in safe custody. In the
first place they were to house young persons who, because many of
them would not subsequently be sentenced to imprisonment or some
other form of custody, ought to avoid the experience of prison either
before trial or sentence. Implicit in such an objective would seem
to be the view that remand centres should provide a regime which
would better safeguard the rights and freedoms of remand and trial
prisoners than could be achieved in local prisons. Second, remand
centres were to provide a better service to the courts so as to
enable them to arrive at more 'scientific' sentencing decisions. Our
evidence suggests that Winchester remand centre has done little more
than to duplicate the regime and relationships of Winchester local
prison, albeit in somewhat superior physical surroundings. Apart
from his separation from adult convicted persons, the rights of the
unconvicted prisoner were no better protected in the remand centre
than in the prison. And if the provision and use of resources, both
material and human, is any guide, then Prison Department does not
appear to have paid much more than lip-service to the diagnostic
function of the remand centre. We give further consideration to the
implications of these findings in chapter 6 following a review of the
careers of the remand centre prisoners which is the subject of the
next chapter.

Chapter 5

CUSTODIAL CAREERS ON REMAND

Some of the most interesting questions about the operation of criminal justice systems today are concerned with the way in which
earlier decisions in a given case may influence subsequent disposal.
The questions are not just academic. Whether or not a decision to
remand or commit a person to custody itself increases the likelihood
of conviction or the passing of a custodial sentence is as important
for any individual defendant as it is for the administrators who
have to plan the use of available resources. By the time a defendant appears in court he has already travelled some distance
along a 'career path' in which a number of decisions have been made,
most notably by the police. But only after his appearance in court
can he be launched upon a custodial career involving the establishments run by Prison Department. How long he spends in them and what
he does whilst he is there will be consequential for him and his
family. How many people are committed to these establishments, for
how long and for what purposes will be no less consequential for
Prison Department.

Rather few data are available from official sources which would
permit some calculation of the way in which trial outcomes are
influenced by earlier events in the judicial process. And it is
often by no means easy to estimate what would be the consequences
for different parts of the penal system if changes in any of the
existing procedures were introduced. In part these problems arise
from the difficulty of linking the various official statistics to
formulate a picture of the careers of individuals who pass through
the system. In the present chapter we hope to throw some light on
custodial career patterns through an examination of the records of
persons passing through Winchester remand centre. But first it will
be helpful if we illustrate some of the difficulties of working from
the official statistics.

There is no official source where information on the total annual
number of persons remanded or committed in custody is collected together. The Criminal Statistics report the use of custody only on
sentence or in committal proceedings. Thus in 1972 we know that of
373,388 persons proceeded against for an indictable offence, 48,942
persons or 13.1 per cent were committed to crown courts for trial;
and of these 11,193 or 22.9 per cent were committed in custody (Cmnd

5402, 1973, Table 1a). As might be expected a much smaller proportion was committed for trial for non-indictable offences. In
1972 9,646 persons were committed, or 0.5 per cent of the 1,569,162
persons against whom proceedings were taken. But even here 16.9
per cent of those committed, some 1,630 persons, were held in
custody. Again as one might expect, a higher proportion of persons
over 21 years was committed for trial for the more serious indictable offences than persons between 17 and 21 years - 16.6 per cent
against 15.4 per cent; although this position was reversed for
non-indictable offences where the proportions were 0.6 per cent and
1.2 per cent respectively. But of particular interest for those
concerned with planning the use of available resources was the fact
that it was the younger age group which provided the greater proportion of persons committed in custody: 25 per cent against 22 per
cent for indictable offences and 21.1 per cent against 15.7 per cent
for non-indictables (Cmnd 5402, 1973, Tables 1b and c).

Unfortunately the Criminal Statistics do not report the use of
custody during summary proceedings. Nor do they give the number of
persons who were subsequently committed for trial but who had
already been remanded in custody before committal. However we know
from the Prison Department Statistical Tables that in 1972 there
were 44,501 receptions of untried persons (Cmnd 5489, 1973). If
11,193 were committed in custody awaiting trial at a higher court
for indictable offences and a further 1,630 were similarly committed for non-indictable offences, we may presume that the remaining 31,678 were remanded in custody by magistrates' courts - and
that this figure probably included some persons who were subsequently committed for trial.

The official statistics for convicted but unsentenced prisoners
are similarly inadequate. The Criminal Statistics report the
numbers of persons committed to crown courts for sentence under
section 28 and 29 of the Magistrates' Courts Act 1952, but since the
Criminal Justice Act 1967 introduced the possibility of using bail
for sentence committals it is no longer possible to say how many of
the persons in these categories were held in custody. Moreover the
Criminal Statistics give no information regarding the use of remands
in custody prior to sentence under other provisions either by
magistrates' courts or by crown courts. The Prison Department Statistical Tables do report the annual number of convicted but unsentenced receptions, but apart from those received under section 26
of the Magistrates' Courts Act for medical reports, do not indicate
the provisions under which persons are detained. It is thus not
possible to say by which court persons have been remanded in custody.

The Prison Department Statistical Tables provide us with information about the outcome of proceedings for persons who are held in
custody before trial, and for persons who are held in custody
pending sentence. They also indicate the degree of overlap between
these groups - that is how many persons first received into custody
before trial are subsequently received again prior to sentence. But
they tell us nothing about the length of time untried and unsentenced prisoners spend in custody, even though both the Criminal
Statistics and the Prison Department publish the distribution of
sentenced prisoners by length of sentence. A simple assessment can

be made, however, as to the average duration of pre-trial and pre-sentence custody by relating the annual reception figures to the average daily population using the formula:
duration = (ADP x 365) ÷ Receptions. Table 5.1 shows that these calculations yield some surprising results for recent years.

TABLE 5.1   Average duration of custody for male and female untried and unsentenced prisoners

Year	Males			Females		
	Recep.	ADP	Mean days	Recep.	ADP	Mean days
Untried prisoners						
1960	26,229	1,388	19	1,496	44	11
1967	38,049	1,693	16	2,213	99	16
1968	38,274	1,836	18	2,229	99	16
1969	42,159	2,333	20	2,108	113	20
1970	44,733	2,776	23	2,492	137	20
1971	48,781	2,840	21	2,972	147	18
1972*	44,891	2,923	24	2,827	133	17
Unsentenced prisoners						
1960	9,869	590	22	1,281	63	18
1967	19,598	1,190	22	1,598	84	19
1968	17,905	1,145	23	1,222	75	22
1969	20,563	1,345	24	1,293	77	22
1970	22,102	1,525	25	1,386	90	24
1971	22,240	1,524	25	1,401	85	22
1972*	19,582	1,560	29	1,086	81	27

Source: Summary of reception and population figures from the Prison Department Statistical Tables, 1960-72.
* Figures for 1972 have been adjusted to include persons remanded under section 26 of the Magistrates' Courts Act 1952 with untried prisoners as they had been for earlier years.
   Mean duration of stay calculated by the formula:
   duration = (ADP x 365) ÷ Receptions and expressed to the nearest day.

   From Table 5.1 it seems that the average period spent in custody by both untried and unsentenced prisoners in 1972 was considerably longer than that spent by their predecessors in 1960. Time spent in custody remained rather shorter for untried prisoners than for un-sentenced prisoners, and for females rather than males, throughout the period. None the less the increases from 1960 to 1972 were dramatic. Untried males and females spent respectively five and six days longer in custody, unsentenced males a week longer, and un-sentenced females nine days longer - or half as much again as they would have spent in 1960. There does not appear to be any obvious explanation, other than pressure on the courts, for these increases which are all the more disturbing because of the efforts in recent years to reduce both the use and duration of pre-trial and pre-

sentence custody. Indeed 1972 was the first year of operation of
the Courts Act 1971, under which it was hoped that the reorganisation of the courts would lead to a speeding up in the hearing of
cases. Of course, it cannot be concluded from these data that no
speeding up of the process has taken place. The full effect of the
Act would be unlikely to appear in the first year, and it may well
be that the early impact of reorganisation was on cases involving
persons who were remanded or committed on bail. It is also important to note that some improvement did occur in 1971 for both
male and female untried prisoners and for female unsentenced prisoners, while the line was at least held for unsentenced males. Unfortunately the improvement was sustained into the following year
only for untried females, all other groups reaching new peaks in
1972. In the circumstances it is difficult to know quite how to
interpret the comment by Prison Department in its Annual Report for
1972 that 'the periods which prisoners spend in custody awaiting
trial have generally shown some reduction, although there are continuing difficulties in London' (Cmnd 5375, 1973, para.74).
    However suggestive these estimates may be they tell us very
little about individual prisoners and their experience of custody at
different stages in their careers. And this is a gap in our
knowledge which has only partly been filled by research. The most
exhaustive investigation so far has been by the Home Office Research
Unit and their report 'Time Spent Awaiting Trial' (HORU, 1960), was
primarily concerned with careers prior to conviction. Although some
attention has been paid to careers following conviction, neither the
Home Office study nor subsequent studies (Bottomley, 1970; Davies,
1971; M.King, 1971) have been able to relate the separate stages
of an individual's career. In an attempt to link up the custodial
elements in the various stages of careers on remand, we carried out
a census of all prisoners held in Winchester remand centre during
the first three months of 1971. Of course, some of these prisoners
had been first received in 1970 while others, received for the first
time before the end of March 1971, were not tried, convicted or
sentenced until later in the year. We therefore attempted to
collect data retrospectively for some prisoners, and followed up
others, until we had obtained a complete record for all persons held
in the centre between 31 December 1970 and 31 March 1971, and which
covered the period from the time each prisoner first appeared before
a magistrates' court until he was acquitted or until sentence had
been passed.
    Remand centres, like local prisons, receive and contain persons
in all the main legal categories - untried, unsentenced, sentenced
and civil. They none the less handle fewer individual persons than
might commonly be supposed because the same individuals frequently
pass through two or more legal categories within a fairly short
period of time, in connection with the same offence. And the same
person may be received more than once during a single year in connection with different offences. According to the statistics
routinely recorded by staff in Winchester remand centre there were
730 receptions during January, February and March 1971. However, it
was clear that this routine procedure involved the recording of a
new reception each time a prisoner was received under a new order,
even if he remained in the same legal category. We were concerned

to establish the number of persons actually involved, and the number of times they were received in different legal categories. Our census data revealed that 247 persons were held in custody during this period. For ten of these persons we were unable to ascertain whether they were held as untried or unsentenced prisoners, although we know from the brevity of their stay that they were only received in one and not both of these categories. The remainder were involved in 151 receptions before trial, 121 receptions awaiting sentence, and 91 receptions after sentence. There were thus effectively 373 receptions under the various legal categories during this period although obviously some persons were detained in all three categories.

The circumstances under which a person may be held in a remand centre are many and varied. The extremes which were to be found within our census data may best be conveyed by two examples. A 20 year-old youth was remanded in custody by a local magistrates' court on a charge of burglary. The court, which may only remand in custody for eight clear days at a time, remanded the accused in custody on three occasions and he spent a total of nineteen days in the centre before being tried. Found guilty of burglary the youth was again remanded in custody this time for medical and social reports under section 14.3 of the Magistrates' Courts Act 1952: a further twenty-one days were spent in the centre. Having studied the reports the magistrates decided that their sentencing powers were inadequate and committed the prisoner to quarter sessions for sentence under section 29 of the Magistrates' Courts Act 1952. After spending a further twenty-six days in the centre the prisoner appeared at quarter sessions for sentence where the judge concluded that the case required further consideration. The case was adjourned for seven days, again spent in custody, after which the prisoner was committed to Broadmoor under section 60 of the Mental Health Act 1959. Two more days were passed in the remand centre, however, before transport to Broadmoor became available. This prisoner thus spent seventy-five consecutive nights in the remand centre having been received from a court under a new order on no less than seven different occasions under five separate legislative provisions. His career as a prisoner passed through three legal categories - untried, unsentenced and sentenced. This case may be contrasted with a youth who was accused of robbery, spent five months on bail awaiting trial and who, having been found guilty and sentenced to borstal training, then spent seven days in the remand centre awaiting transfer to a borstal.

At the time of our research in 1971 all accused persons were - as they are today - brought before a magistrates' court in the first instance. Thereafter there were five possible career paths which they might follow, any of which might involve them in a period spent in custody. First, the accused might be both tried and sentenced in summary proceedings before a magistrates' court. Second, persons might be committed to a court of quarter sessions for sentence after summary trial proceedings. Third, in cases where the offence for which they had been summarily convicted involved a breach of a sentence imposed earlier by an assize court, persons could be committed to an assize court for sentence. Fourth and fifth, in cases where the offence was considered to be sufficiently serious that it must be tried by jury, or where the accused could and did elect to be tried by jury, both trial and sentence would be carried out either at quarter sessions or at a court of assize. In practice courts of quarter sessions dealt mainly with property offences, while assize courts, which accounted for less than a quarter of all higher court trials, tended to hear cases involving offences against the person and the more serious cases of fraud. Since 1971 the replacement of courts of assize and quarter sessions by a single court, the crown court, has meant that these five career paths have been reduced to three. However, although the census data that we report below were collected some years ago there is no reason yet to believe that the patterns of custody that they reveal will have changed significantly in the interval.

The only item of information which we were able to collect for all 247 individuals in our census was age, and the distribution is given in Table 5.2. One prisoner, who was 21 years of age, was mistakenly held in the remand centre for one night only before being

TABLE 5.2 Age distribution of persons held in Winchester remand centre: 31 December 1970 to 31 March 1971

Age in years	No.of persons	%
14	4 ⎫	
15	7 ⎬	10.9
16	16 ⎭	
17	51 ⎫	
18	56 ⎪	
19	55 ⎬	89.1
20	57 ⎭	
21	1	
Total, all ages 247		100.0

transferred to the main prison. It is worth noting that the proportion of persons in our census who were under 17 years of age, 10.9 per cent was very similar to the proportion of receptions under this age reported in the Prison Department Statistics for 1971, 12.8 per cent. This suggests that, while there will always be more receptions than persons actually involved in custody, the receptions data provided by Prison Department none the less give a fair indication of the proportions of persons in different age categories receiving custody, if not the actual numbers of such persons.

We had to exclude 14 individuals from all further analysis because of lack of information, and the detailed reasons for this are given in the notes to Table 5.3 below. In Table 5.3 we report the numbers and proportions of the remaining 233 prisoners in the remand centre census who followed each of the five career paths which we have outlined. Nearly two-thirds of all prisoners passing through the centre were tried, and rather more than a third were

sentenced, by magistrates' courts. It follows that the higher
courts of assize and quarter sessions were then responsible for
sentencing almost two thirds of these prisoners even though they had
tried only just over one-third of them. Most of the higher court
cases were disposed of by the quarter sessions who tried five cases
for every two tried by assize courts, and sentenced five for every
one sentenced by the assizes. The new crown courts will have inherited a similar role and a similar burden of cases to the assize
courts and quarter sessions combined.

TABLE 5.3   Career patterns of prisoners held in Winchester remand
centre: 31 December 1970 to 31 March 1971

Career path	Court of first appearance	Trial court	Sentencing court	Prisoners	
				No.	%
1	MC	MC	MC	88	37.8
2	MC	MC	QS	63	27.0
3	MC	MC	ASS	1	0.4
4	MC	QS	QS	57	24.5
5	MC	ASS	ASS	24	10.3
				233	100.0

Note: 247 prisoners were held in the centre during the census
period, 14 of whom could not be included in the above schema
nor in any subsequent analysis, for the following reasons:
(i)   5 prisoners were received from Channel Island courts
having been sentenced to borstal training and were held
prior to transfer to a borstal establishment. Nothing
was known of their earlier career.
(ii)   5 prisoners were transferred from the remand centre
after such short stays that no further information
could be found concerning them: 4 were transferred to
Pucklechurch remand centre and 1 to the main prison
after a mistake about his age was discovered.
(iii) 3 aliens were held for three days awaiting deportation.
(iv)   1 prisoner, having been held for 7 days as an untried
prisoner was given bail but subsequently failed to sur-
render to it. No further information was available
concerning him.

Because our data were drawn from a census of remand centre
prisoners and not from a census or sample of court decisions, it is
not possible to say what proportion of cases handled by the courts
served by Winchester remand centre resulted in pre-sentence custody
of one kind or another. None the less some limited comparisons can
be made with previous studies over the amount of time spent in
custody before trial and sentence. To do so we had to eliminate 14
prisoners from our census who were only received into custody for
the first time after they had been sentenced by higher courts, and a

further 5 prisoners for whom our information on the various stages
of their careers was incomplete. All subsequent analysis is
therefore based on a population of 214 persons, of whom 93 experienced pre-trial custody only, 64 experienced custody only while
awaiting sentence, and 57 who experienced both. It is clear from a
comparison with Table D22 of the Prison Department Statistical
Tables for 1971 (Cmnd 5156, 1972) that the pattern of receptions
into Winchester remand centre was broadly comparable to the national
picture. Of the total receptions at Winchester, other than those on
sentence, 55.4 per cent were received before conviction and 44.6 per
cent after conviction compared to 59 per cent and 41 per cent respectively for persons under 21 received into prisons and remand
centres generally. The proportion of persons held only after trial
was again similar: 29.9 per cent for Winchester and 28.8 per cent
nationally. However, a rather higher proportion of persons received
into Winchester before trial was also received into custody after
conviction - 26.6 per cent as against 20.7 per cent nationally -
with a consequently lower proportion held only before trial - 43.5
per cent compared to 50.5 per cent. This slight over-representation
of the group held before and after trial at Winchester is unlikely
to affect the calculations in this chapter about the work load of
the remand centre, nor the inferences to be drawn from them for
the system as a whole.

Both the Home Office Research Unit (1960) study and Bottomley
(1970) indicated that significant differences in the duration of
remand and committal proceedings were to be found between large and
small and urban and rural courts. In general these differences were
attributed to variations in the burden of work between courts and to
the frequency of court sittings. Winchester remand centre served a
variety of courts ranging from the larger magistrates' courts in
Portsmouth, Bournemouth and Southampton to the smaller rural benches
at Ringwood and Alresford. And similarly with higher courts. While
Hampshire Assizes was considered to be one of the larger courts of
assize, Hampshire and Salisbury Quarter Sessions were respectively
only medium and small courts (for classification of courts, see
HORU, 1960, Appendix B). With a total population of 214 persons,
the number of persons received into Winchester remand centre from
any one court during our census period was small, and no adequate
investigation of differences between individual courts was possible.
However, a comparison between persons received from the three
largest magistrates' courts at Portsmouth, Bournemouth and
Southampton, with those received from the remaining twenty magistrates' courts represented in the census revealed no significant
differences in the duration of custody at any stage in the penal
process.

Previous studies have indicated that about 60 per cent of persons
remanded by magistrates' courts before trial are remanded in
custody. Bottomley (1970, p.28) reported that the average duration
of custody prior to trial for those persons who were not successful
in being released on bail was eight days, while persons remanded on
bail took between fourteen and sixteen days to come to trial.
Bottomley's figure for remands in custody was somewhat lower than
that reported by the Home Office Research Unit (HORU, 1960, p.26) of
9.8 days. In fact these figures are not strictly comparable because

Bottomley included the time spent in custody prior to committal of
those persons committed by magistrates to higher courts for trial,
although this is unlikely to make very much difference. Our
findings are similar to the earlier study, the average custodial
period before trial for persons in our census remanded by magistrates and dealt with summarily being 10.5 days.

In Table 5.4 we present the mean periods spent in custody before
trial for those persons who received part-bail and those who were
continuously detained, together with the mean periods spent awaiting
sentence.   Although the mean pre-trial detention period for all
groups was 16.9 days, it can be seen from Table 5.4 that the period
was considerably shorter (10.7 days) for those getting part-bail
than for those who were held continuously in custody (18.6 days).
The mean time in custody after conviction pending sentence was 22.6
days. However there were considerable variations between one career
path and another.

TABLE 5.4 Mean periods spent in pre-trial and pre-sentence custody
by prisoners held in Winchester remand centre: 31 December 1970 to
31 March 1971

Career path	Pre-trial custody				Await sentence		Total custody	
	Part-bail		Continuous custody					
	No.	Days	No.	Days	No.	Days	No.	Days
1 MC–MC–MC	6	5.8	62	10.5	39	21.0	88	17.1
2 MC–MC–QS	1	7.0	28	12.5	60	30.3	60	36.3
3 MC–MC–ASS	–	–	1	7.0	1	12.0	1	19.0
4 MC–QS–QS	16	9.3	24	43.3	9	5.2	46	26.8
5 MC–ASS–ASS	9	16.9	3	48.0	12	2.9	19	17.4
	32	10.7	118	18.6	121	22.6	214	24.6

Not surprisingly, unless a prisoner was fortunate enough to be released on bail for some period, he was likely to spend most time in
custody before trial if he was both tried and sentenced by a higher
court, especially an assize court, and least time in custody if he
was dealt with in summary proceedings. The largest group brought
before a higher court consisted of persons committed to quarter
sessions for sentence and it was this group which spent by far the
longest period in custody awaiting sentence. Indeed when custody
before and after trial were taken together they spent even longer in
custody than persons who were both tried and sentenced by higher
courts, for prisoners on these career paths were rarely detained for
long once they had been convicted. However, it should be noted that
the 'total custody' column in Table 5.4 gives average figures for
the total time in pre-trial custody and custody pending sentence

spent by all prisoners in each career path. It does not distinguish between persons who experienced only one form of custody either as untried or unsentenced prisoners, and persons who experienced both. In Table 5.5 we look more closely at the 57 prisoners who were detained both before and after conviction, and the amount of time they spent in custody. For each career path these prisoners, of course, had longer periods in total custody than the average for their groups.

TABLE 5.5 Mean periods spent in custody by prisoners detained both before and after conviction

	No.	Days before trial	Days awaiting sentence	Total days
MC-MC-MC	19	9.5	23.1	32.6
MC-MC-QS	29	12.3	30.6	42.9
MC-MC-ASS	1	7.0	12.0	19.0
MC-QS-QS	3	27.3	9.7	37.0
MC-ASS-ASS	5	15.2	3.0	18.2
	57	12.3	24.3	36.6

In the paragraphs below we examine the five career patterns that we found in our census in greater detail.

PERSONS TRIED AND SENTENCED IN MAGISTRATES' COURTS

There were 88 persons in our census who were both tried and sentenced by magistrates' courts. They would be recorded as the reception of 68 untried prisoners (B,C,D,E and G in table 5.6) and 39 unsentenced prisoners (A,C,F and G), although in reality there were 49 persons held before trial only (B,D and E), 19 persons who were held both before and after conviction (C and G), and 20 who were held only while awaiting sentence (A and F). Actually the situation was rather more complicated than that because 3 of those held in custody before trial only, and 3 who were held both before and after trial, were detained for shorter periods, sometimes no more than a day or so, before being released on bail. In Table 5.6 we have tried to set out as clearly as possible the relationship between custody before and after conviction and the eventual trial outcomes for all 88 persons in this career group.

Less than a fifth of this group were eventually returned to custody after sentence. Only 2 of the 20 prisoners who were in receipt of bail for part of the period prior to trial or sentence were finally sentenced to custody by the magistrates, while 16 were given other sentences and a further 2 were found not guilty. Proportionately twice as many of those held continuously in custody either before trial or for reports before sentence or both, 15 out of 68, were again incarcerated after sentence, although here too 53 persons or nearly four-fifths of the total were given non-custodial sentences. Not surprisingly it was to the group held continuously in custody both before and after conviction that most custodial sentences were awarded.

TABLE 5.6   Pre-trial and pre-sentence custody in relation to outcome for persons tried and sentenced by magistrates' courts

	Position prior to sentence			Outcome		
	Pre-trial	Await sentence	No.	Not guilty	Non-custody	Custody
A	Bail	Custody	2	0	2	0
B	Custody/bail	Bail	3	2	1	0
C	Custody/bail	Custody	3	0	3	0
D	Custody	Bail	12	0	10	2
E	Custody	No remand	34	0	30	4
F	No remand	Custody	18	0	14	4
G	Custody	Custody	16	0	9	7
		Totals	88	2	69	17

Note: Until 1971 persons detained under section 26 of the Magistrates' Courts Act 1952 were arbitrarily recorded in the official statistics as 'untried prisoners' although magistrates could use this power both before and after conviction. Since 1972 these persons have been recorded, equally arbitrarily, as 'unsentenced prisoners'. In this and succeeding tables we have recorded section 26 prisoners either as 'pre-trial' or as 'awaiting sentence' depending on when the remand in custody was actually made.

Although there were more prisoners who experienced pre-trial custody than experienced custody pending sentence - 68 against 39 including the 19 who experienced both - they took up proportionately very much less of the remand centre's time and facilities. Many of those held before trial were soon released on bail and the average time in pre-trial custody was 10.1 days. Most remands for reports prior to sentence under sections 14.3 and 26 of the Magistrates' Courts Act 1952, however, were for either 14 or 21 days although 4 prisoners were held for up to four weeks and 4 were held between five and eight weeks. The average period spent in custody awaiting sentence was 21 days. Thus of the 1,508 man-days spent in the remand centre by the 88 people tried and sentenced by magistrates' courts only 686 or 45.6 per cent were spent awaiting trial while 820 or 54.4 per cent were spent during the preparation of pre-sentence reports. This, of course, wholly in keeping with the supposed diagnostic function of remand centres. But it is incumbent upon those who believe in the diagnostic value of these reports to demonstrate that such medical and social assessments could not

equally well be prepared while the offender is at liberty, especially in view of the fact that 72 per cent of those on whom reports
were prepared during custody were subsequently released into the
community on sentence. This compares with 78 per cent of the
prisoners held before trial who were not returned to custody on
sentence. If the 28 persons held by magistrates between trial and
sentence and who were subsequently given non-custodial sentences,
had been investigated in the community instead of in custody, there
would have been a saving of 580 man-days. This would represent
exactly 11 per cent of the work of the remand centre as this is
measured by time devoted to pre-trial and pre-sentence custody; and
we return to this matter later in the chapter.

That being said, it is important to point out that for this
career group, the largest in our census, time spent in custody bore
an equitable relationship to eventual custodial outcome: the two
persons found not guilty were detained for one and seven days respectively, those who received non-custodial sentences were detained
on average for 16.4 days, and those who were sentenced to prison,
borstal or detention centres spent on average 21.8 days in the
remand centre before being sentenced.

PERSONS COMMITTED TO HIGHER COURTS FOR SENTENCE

After eliminating 3 persons on whom we had insufficient data there
were 60 persons in our census who were found guilty at magistrates'
courts and then committed, under sections 28 or 29 of the Magistrates' Courts Act 1952, to quarter sessions for sentence. And
there was one further person who was committed to a court of assize
in respect of a breach of a probation order originally imposed by
that court. For obvious reasons we will focus on those committed to
quarter sessions.

There were 29 untried receptions (I and K in Table 5.7) and 60
unsentenced prisoners (H,I,J, and K). All 29 of the untried re-
appeared as unsentenced prisoners where they were joined by 9 who
had been on bail prior to conviction and 22 who had been remanded
only after they had been found guilty. In Table 5.7 we summarise
the relationships between custody before and after conviction and
eventual trial outcomes for all 60 persons in our census who were
committed to sessions for sentence.

This group as a whole stood a much greater chance of receiving a
custodial sentence than the group dealt with by magistrates alone -
76.7 per cent compared with 19.3 per cent. This is not surprising
since the main reason for a committal for sentence was that the
magistrates felt their powers to be inadequate. However there were
some differences in outcome according to the degree of custody experienced before sentence. Only 3 out of 5 of those remanded wholly
or partly on bail before conviction were sentenced to custody, compared with 4 out of 5 of those who had not been remanded before
trial but who were detained in custody after conviction, and 9 out
of 10 of those held continuously in custody both before and after
trial.

Persons held in the remand centre both before and after trial
were often detained for long periods. Twelve persons, a fifth of

the whole career group, were held for more than 50 days in all, and 2 for more than 100 days. One person spent a total of 120 days in custody, the equivalent of a six months' prison sentence with full remission, before being placed on probation. The situation was complicated by the fact that sometimes the magistrates decided first to remand the prisoner for reports and then to commit for sentence: the 12 prisoners dealt with in this way spent an average of 57.7 days in custody.

TABLE 5.7   Pre-trial and pre-sentence custody in relation to outcome for persons committed to quarter sessions for sentence

Position prior to sentence		Outcome		
Pre-trial	Await sentence	No.	Non-custody	Custody
H Bail	Custody	9	4	5
I Custody/bail	Custody	1	-	1
J No remand	Custody	22	7	15
K Custody	Custody	28	3	25
		60	14	46

    The mean time spent in custody before trial was 12.3 days and the mean time in custody pending sentence was 30.3 days. Since there were many more prisoners in this career group experiencing custody while awaiting sentence (60) than while awaiting trial (29) they used nearly six times as much of the resources of the remand centre. Persons who were committed for sentence accounted for 1,819 man-days while awaiting sentence and 356 man-days while awaiting trial. This was, of course, only to be expected given the nature of this career path. So, perhaps, was the fact that the persons who eventually received non-custodial sentences spent rather less time in custody on average than those who were sentenced to some form of detention - 28.1 days as against 38.7 days - largely because they were more likely to have received bail before trial and less likely to have been remanded for reports before committal.

PERSONS TRIED AND SENTENCED IN COURTS OF QUARTER SESSIONS

There were 46 prisoners left in our census who were tried and sentenced at quarter sessions after we had eliminated 9 who were received into the remand centre for the first time only after sentence and 2 on whom we had incomplete information. The 40 untried receptions (M,N,O,P and Q in Table 5.8) and 9 unsentenced receptions (L,N and Q), were accounted for by 37 persons who were held before trial only (M,O and P), 3 who were held both before trial and while awaiting sentence (N and Q) and 6 who were held only while awaiting sentence (L).

Almost half of this career group received bail at some stage in the legal process, but they experienced one of two quite distinct patterns of custody. Most were remanded in custody by a magistrates' court prior to a committal for trial on bail, and of these 12.5 per cent were found not guilty and 56.3 per cent received custodial sentences. But 5 persons, who had been bailed before and during their trial, were remanded in custody while their cases were adjourned for sentence - 4 of them for one day only and 1 for three days. None of these was subsequently sentenced to any form of detention, 2 being placed on probation, 2 fined and 1 conditionally discharged. One other person who had been in receipt of bail was given a custodial sentence after being held in the remand centre for eleven days while judgment was respited. Most investigations into bail proceedings have considered the question as to whether pre-trial or pre-sentence custody is used by the courts with an intention to punish, or at least whether it is considered at a later stage to have served as such. In the case of these 5 'prisoners' it is hard to find any other interpretation than that they were given 'a taste of prison' as a warning for what would happen next time. Once again we set out the relationship between custody before and after conviction and eventual sentence in tabular form in Table 5.8.

TABLE 5.8   Pre-trial and pre-sentence custody in relation to outcome for persons tried and sentenced by courts of quarter sessions

	Position prior to sentence			Outcome		
	Pre-trial	Await sentence	No.	Not guilty	Non-custody	Custody
L	Bail	Custody	6	-	5	1
M	Custody/bail	No remand	15	2	5	8
N	Custody/bail	Custody	1	-	-	1
O	Custody	Bail	1	-	-	1
P	Custody	No remand	21	1	5	15
Q	Custody	Custody	2	-	2	-
			46	3	17	26

The overall period spent in custody by this career group averaged 26.8 days, although 12 prisoners spent more than 50 days in the remand centre. Unlike the career groups we have considered so far, this group spent very much less time in custody while awaiting sentence than it did before trial - partly because some reports would have been prepared during the committal period. In fact of the total time spent in custody by this group 1,187 days or 96.2 per cent occurred before trial, an average of 29.7 days for the 40 prisoners experiencing it. Only 47 days, or 3.8 per cent, were spent after conviction at an average of 5.2 days for the 9 persons concerned.

Two of the 3 persons not found guilty by the quarter sessions fared rather less well than their counterparts who were not found guilty by the magistrates, and spent 25 days and 44 days in the remand centre. The third was released after spending one night in the centre. The average total period in custody for the 17 prisoners who were not eventually detained on sentence was 16.5 days compared to 34.0 days for the 26 prisoners who were finally sentenced to detention.

PERSONS TRIED AND SENTENCED AT ASSIZES

Five prisoners who were sentenced by assize courts to borstal training were received into the remand centre only after sentence while awaiting transfer. When these were eliminated from the study we were left with 19 persons in our census who were tried and sentenced by courts of assize. They accounted for 12 untried receptions (S,T, U and V in Table 5.9) and 12 unsentenced receptions (R,T and V), although in fact 7 persons were held only before trial (S and U), 7 were held only after conviction (R), and 5 appeared in both categories (T and V). We should say at once that, apart from the very small numbers involved in this career path, interpretation is further complicated by the fact that 13 of the prisoners were involved in three separate affray trials, each of which proved to be both complex and prolonged. However, for what it is worth, persons held in custody for a short confinement before sentence by courts of assize were all sentenced to custody, unlike those dealt with by quarter sessions, as can be seen from Table 5.9.

TABLE 5.9 Pre-trial and pre-sentence custody in relation to outcome for persons tried and sentenced by courts of assize

	Position prior to sentence			Outcome		
	Pre-trial	Await sentence	No.	Not guilty	Non-custody	Custody
R	Bail	Custody	7	–	–	7
S	Custody/bail	No remand	5	–	2	3
T	Custody/bail	Custody	4	–	–	4
U	Custody	Bail	2	–	2	–
V	Custody	Custody	1	–	–	1
			19	0	4	15

The average total time in custody for this group was 17.4 days, with 3 prisoners spending more than 50 days in the remand centre. But, as with persons tried and sentenced by quarter sessions, persons dealt with by the assizes spent much less time in custody awaiting sentence than they did awaiting trial - presumably for the same reason that reports prepared during the committal period obvi-

ated the need for a further remand for enquiries before sentence.
Of the total time spent in custody by the assize court group 296
days or 89.4 per cent occurred before trial, an average of 24.7 days
for the 12 persons involved. Only 35 days, or 10.6 per cent, were
spent in detention awaiting sentence at an average of 2.9 days for
the 12 prisoners who experienced it.

Persons tried and sentenced by the assize courts provided the
only career path in our census where, on average, prisoners who were
eventually given a non-custodial sentence actually spent more time
in the remand centre, 32 days, than did prisoners who were eventually sentenced to a prison, borstal or detention centre, 13.5 days.
However, it should be repeated that the numbers involved were small,
and that much of this difference appears to have resulted from the
court's decision to deal with the participants in one of the affray
cases by non-custodial sentences only after extensive enquiries had
been carried out during a long committal period.

THE COURTS AND THE WORK OF THE REMAND CENTRE

In Table 5.10 we give full details of the sentences received by all
persons in our census who spent some time in the remand centre
either before or after trial or both. Two per cent were not found
guilty. Exactly half the remainder were given non-custodial
sentences, and half of these were dealt with either by discharge or
fine which required no further supervision from the criminal justice
system. But, as we have seen, considerable differences were found
between one career path and another. Only a fifth of the persons
tried and sentenced by magistrates' courts and held as either untried or unsentenced prisoners subsequently received a custodial
sentence, compared with four-fifths of those dealt with at a court
of assize. This contrast, however, is somewhat misleading. Persons
sentenced by magistrates should probably be considered in conjunction with persons that the magistrates have committed to higher
courts for sentence. For in these cases the magistrates have, in
effect, made a sentence proposal by suggesting that their own powers
were inadequate. Viewed in this light some three-quarters of magistrates' proposals were confirmed through the imposition of custody
by a higher court. Moreover, as we have said, the numbers dealt
with by assizes in our census were small, and were derived largely
from related cases. It would perhaps be more appropriate,
therefore, to combine the assize court group with the quarter
sessions group for comparative purposes. In that case just over
three-fifths of the persons tried by higher courts were sentenced
to custody, compared with a little more than two-fifths of those
tried by the magistrates.

Even so, with half of all the persons who were in custody before
sentence not experiencing it after sentence, it is reasonable to
examine the resources which they used and to ask whether the ends of
justice could have been met in a manner involving greater economy
for the state and greater freedom for the individual. In Table 5.11
we have tried to show how the career groups we have discussed in
this chapter contributed to the work of the remand centre. There
are several ways in which the work of an institution might be as-

TABLE 5.10 Court disposal for all persons held before trial or sentence in Winchester remand centre: 31 December 1970 to 31 March 1971

		Not guilty or case dismissed	Non-custodial sentence				Custodial sentence			
			Condit. or abs. disch.	Fine	Probation or care order	Susp. sent.	App. school	Det. centre	Borstal (inc. recall)	Prison or det. under M.H.A.
MC–MC–MC	No.	2	9	29	28	3	–	7	7	3
	% 100.0	2.3			78.4				19.3	
MC–MC–QS	No.	–	–	3	11	–	2	4	36	4
	% 100.0	0.0			23.3				76.7	
MC–MC–ASS	No.	–	–	–	–	–	–	–	–	1
	% 100.0	0.0			0.0				100.0	
MC–QS–QS	No.	3	1	4	12	–	–	4	17	5
	% 100.0	6.5			37.0				56.5	
MC–ASS–ASS	No.	–	–	2	2	–	–	3	5	7
	% 100.0	0.0			21.1				78.9	
All courts	Total 214	5	10	38	53	3	2	18	65	20
	% 100.0	2.3			48.6				49.1	

sessed. We could, for example, have looked at the amount of staff
time devoted to receptions and discharges and record-keeping and so
on. But perhaps the simplest and probably the most effective index
for present purposes is the number of man-days of custody devoted to
the various categories of prisoner held. Accordingly we have set
out in Table 5.11 the actual number of days spent in pre-trial and
pre-sentence custody by each career group according to the eventual
outcome of sentence. And we have expressed the number of days for
each group as a proportion of the total number of man-days of
custody for all untried and unsentenced prisoners. This, of course,
excludes that part of the work of the remand centre given over to
the custody of sentenced prisoners, who were actually awaiting
transfer to other institutions and who accounted for about a sixth
of the total work-load of the centre. Sixty-five of the persons
with whom we have been concerned in this chapter were in fact returned to the remand centre having been sentenced to borstal training; 3 more were returned with sentences of imprisonment; and 1
was detained under the Mental Health Act before being transferred to
Broadmoor. To these should be added the 14 prisoners whom we excluded from our census on grounds that they were only received into
the remand centre after they had been sentenced to borstal training.
All told these 83 prisoners were held for a total of 1,224 days
after sentence - an average of about two weeks although individually
periods of post-sentence detention before transfer ranged from 2 to
40 days.

Those persons who were either not found guilty or not subsequently sentenced to custody - about half our census population on whom
we had information - accounted for nearly two-fifths of the total
number of days spent in pre-sentence custody. Even when the time
spent in the centre by sentenced prisoners is added, they still accounted for almost one-third of the total load of Winchester remand
centre. In theory it must be mainly from these groups that savings,
both for individuals and for the prison system, can be expected to
come - for example through the use of bail hostels and bail clinics
or other community-based programmes. But there is some reason to
doubt whether the savings could ever approach this theoretical maximum unless a more radical reappraisal of the use of custody before
trial and sentence is made. And this does not seem likely in the
foreseeable future.

In the first place it must be said that in any system of remands
in custody there will always be some persons who are subsequently
released either as free men and women or on non-custodial
sentences - and that it is by no means easy to know in advance whom
all these persons may be. Second, about one-third of those eventually not found guilty or not sentenced to custody in our census were
committed by the magistrates to higher courts for trial or sentence.
But, as we have seen, committal for trial was frequently made wholly
or partly on bail, and of those committals in custody some two-
thirds eventually did result in a custodial sentence. And the logic
of committals for sentence tends to pre-suppose the probable use of
custody as the final outcome. It therefore seems that if major
inroads into the burden of custodial remands are to be made then
they will have to come from that group dealt with wholly by magistrates' courts. The 88 persons tried and sentenced summarily

TABLE 5.11   Absolute and proportionate use of remand centre facilities, as measured by man-days spent in custody, by prisoners on each career path and for each sentence outcome

		Not guilty or case dismissed	Non-custodial	Custodial	Total
1	MC-MC-MC				
	No.of days	8	1130	370	1508
	Prop.of total	0.1	21.5	7.0	28.6
2	MC-MC-QS				
	No.of days	0	393	1782	2175
	Prop.of total	0	7.5	33.8	41.3
3	MC-MC-ASS				
	No.of days	0	0	19	19
	Prop.of total	0	0	0.4	0.4
4	MC-QS-QS				
	No.of days	70	280	884	1234
	Prop.of total	1.3	5.3	16.8	23.4
5	MC-ASS-ASS				
	No.of days	0	128	203	331
	Prop.of total	0	2.4	3.9	6.3
	All courts				
	No.of days	78	1931	3258	5267
	Prop.of total	1.4	36.7	61.9	100.0

constituted 41 per cent of all the persons received into Winchester remand centre prior to sentence during the census period. The great majority of them, some 71 persons, were either not found guilty or else received a non-custodial sentence. If it were possible to keep these people out of custody, either before conviction or while awaiting sentence, or both, then considerable savings in individual liberty would result, for they constituted exactly one-third of all the persons received in the centre prior to sentence. But since many were held in custody only for short periods the savings in terms of the work of the remand centre itself would be very much less. Between them they accounted for just over one-fifth of the total man-days in the centre before sentence - 10.4 per cent in pretrial detention and 11 per cent in custody awaiting sentence. But when the time devoted to sentenced prisoners is included in the calculation, this group accounted for just one-sixth of the total work load of the centre.

Savings of this magnitude, of course, are well worth having. But it would be quite misleading to suggest that they would go very far towards easing the burden of remand centres even if they could be achieved.

Chapter 6

SUMMARY AND CONCLUSIONS

This study has been concerned with the provisions made for unconvicted and unsentenced prisoners in the penal system. As we
showed in chapter 2 the numbers of persons in these two groups have
increased dramatically over the last decade, such that they now account for a significantly greater proportion of the receptions and
population in Prison Department establishments than formerly. The
increases have been more marked for young persons than for adults.
About half of them do not subsequently receive custodial sentences
when finally disposed of by the courts. Accordingly we undertook a
study of the regimes for unconvicted and unsentenced prisoners in
HM Prison and HM Remand Centre at Winchester. The institutions were
chosen for convenience, in the course of a wider, on-going investigation, rather than for their representativeness but we have no
reason to believe that these establishments differed greatly from
other institutions of their kind run by Prison Department. We began
with a review of current legislation and Prison Department di-
rectives in an attempt to ascertain whether the lives of unconvicted
and unsentenced prisoners are governed by rules other than those
applying to sentenced prisoners. We established that the Prison
Rules do distinguish between unconvicted and convicted prisoners on
nine occasions but that no distinction is made between unsentenced
and sentenced prisoners except that the former are not subject to
restrictions for letters and visits.

Under these Rules, and ostensibly to safeguard their rights, unconvicted prisoners are to be kept separate from convicted prisoners. They may also receive private medical attention, wear their
own clothes, have food sent in, occupy a privately furnished special
cell, be excluded from prison regulation haircuts, choose whether or
not to work, have unlimited letters and visits and have newspapers,
books and certain other items supplied to them from outside the
prison. Data collected from a sample of prisoners in the local
prison at Winchester demonstrated that these Rules, though valuable
in theory, mean little in practice. Some facilities, like special
cells, simply did not exist at Winchester. Other rights were difficult to exercise because their provision was complicated by supplementary regulations in the standing orders and circular instructions
issued by Prison Department or else was subject to staff discretion.

Furthermore, most of the rights to which unconvicted persons were entitled were dependent upon prisoners being able to mobilise financial resources - either their own or those of friends and relations. It was apparent that unconvicted prisoners were rarely in a position to do this. Indeed most unconvicted prisoners in Winchester were unable even to make use of more letters or visits than sentenced prisoners despite the considerable restrictions imposed upon the latter. Presumably this reflected the absence of social contacts which led to their custodial remand in the first place, bearing in mind that the lack of a fixed abode is the most common reason for such a court disposal. Finally the fact that unconvicted prisoners had the right to provide certain things for themselves, even though they were usually unable to take advantage of it, seemed to result in a lack of provision of facilities for them by Prison Department. Thus in Winchester newspapers were supplied by the prison to all but the unconvicted. In summary then the presence of special rights for the unconvicted has not generally served to lighten the burden of custody which they experience and in some respects at least has even tended to make that burden more restrictive than for the convicted.

This assessment was corroborated by a more general analysis of the routine activities which make up the prisoners' regime. Separation of the convicted from the unconvicted in Winchester was achieved largely through the confinement of the latter to their cells: the mean daily time that unconvicted men spent locked in their cells was 21 hours 40 minutes - a good deal longer than convicted men. And for those unconvicted persons who exercised their right not to work there was no alternative to inactivity in their cells. These and other aspects of the regime were reflected in the scores obtained through an application of the measures developed by the Prison Regimes Project. Five scales, block treatment, rigidity, restrictiveness within wings, restrictiveness between wings and supervision, measured degrees of institutional constraint in the routine handling of inmate activities. Although the regime for unconvicted men was found to be less rigid and subject to less supervision than the regime for convicted prisoners, it involved greater restrictiveness both within and between wings and a somewhat higher degree of block treatment. Furthermore there were no significant differences between the untried and the convicted prisoners in the amount of collective responsibility accorded them or the degree of social distance from staff. And although untried prisoners enjoyed more self-responsibility this was offset by the fact that they were the most media-isolated group of prisoners in the establishment.

An evaluation similar to that conducted in the local prison at Winchester was made of the remand centre for young persons which was adjacent to the main prison. We came to the conclusion that the regime provided for unconvicted prisoners in the remand centre was very similar to that found in the local prison. This was hardly surprising because, whatever the intentions of those who framed the legislation creating remand centres, they are in fact governed by the same Statutory Rules as prisons and Prison Department Standing Orders make no distinction between the two types of institution. Prisoners in the remand centre were no more able to exercise their legal rights than were their adult counterparts in the local prison

and were in some respects actually worse off. None wore their own
clothes - clearly as a result of staff direction. None appeared to
have been given any opportunity to refuse the limited amount of work
which was provided. On the credit side the remand centre conferred
some benefits, but they seem marginal enough given the architectural
advantages that it enjoyed when compared with the Victorian building
next door. During the week unconvicted prisoners spent on average a
little over 17 hours per day locked in their cells - 4 hours less
than was the case in the main prison - though there was little
difference between the two institutions at weekends. This reduced
confinement was achieved through the provision of some, not necessarily voluntary, work for all prisoners and limited association
periods and educational classes on alternate evenings.

     Such differences as there were between the remand centre and
local prison at Winchester do not appear to have mitigated the pains
of custody for younger offenders in any significant way apart from
the provision of cleaner and more comfortable buildings. For when
we applied the same measures of regimes to the remand centre we
found generally higher degrees of constraint and lower degrees of
autonomy even than we had found in the local prison. A similar
degree of staff-inmate social distance was recorded in both institutions but the level of media isolation for all prisoners in the
remand centre was higher than for any group of prisoners in any establishment that we have studied in the course of the Prison Regimes
Project. This depressing picture was not leavened by any sign that
the staff at Winchester considered the remand centre to be deficient
in its provision. We found no evidence that the recruitment, training or organisation of staff in the remand centre differed from that
in the main prison. Nor were there any plans under discussion for
possible developments in these areas. In most respects the two establishments had little to distinguish them apart from the age of
their buildings and occupants.

     The data for this study were collected in 1971. Since that time
Prison Department have accepted the recommendations of a project
group set up to study the conditions and treatment of unconvicted
prisoners and introduced a number of measures permitting some relax-
ation of the regimes which we have described (Prison Department
Circular Instruction No.50/1972). At the time of our research most
unconvicted prisoners received their visits in closed conditions,
that is in 'boxes' which physically separated them from their
visitors, although this was not always so and arrangements varied
from prison to prison depending upon the availability of visiting
facilities. Henceforward Prison Department have instructed that
such visits should normally be 'open' although governors may continue closed visits where security considerations are involved or
where the lack of facilities necessitates rationing. Unconvicted
prisoners are now permitted to have their own transistor radios (not
VHF) and battery shavers although in each case they must sign an
undertaking to the effect that they will be subject to periodic
searches and that the items may be withdrawn for unspecified
reasons. Standing Orders now provide that an unconvicted prisoner
may retain a ring, medallion, crucifix, rosary, watch, calendar and
photographs. Unconvicted prisoners may also now receive from
outside a greater range of 'food not in need of preparation' than

was formerly the case. Such food items no longer need constitute a
replacement for a prison meal and they may be paid for out of prison
earnings as well as private cash. The number of letters on which
the prison pays postage has been increased from one to two a week
and these may now be written on personal notepaper although, except
when writing to a child under 16 years, the prisoner must still give
the address of the prison at the top of the page. Finally a prisoner may now receive outside medical attention without referral to
headquarters - though his request may only be granted if the
governor and medical officer consider that it is made on reasonable
grounds.

Circular Instruction 50/1972 also refers to a number of other
matters relating to the unconvicted which are being studied by
Prison Department. Most importantly it is reported that an experi-
ment is being conducted at certain prisons under which prisoners
will be allowed to make telephone calls on urgent personal matters.
And at one prison an effort is being made to extend the scope of
day-time educational and recreational activities which would permit
prisoners to leave their cells. A review is also being made of reception procedures and the circular draws the attention of governors
to the existing rule that prisoners may not be stripped or searched
in the presence of other prisoners - a rule which was several times
honoured in the breach during our own research.

All of these developments are greatly to be welcomed. However it
must be said that they hardly amount to a new charter for the protection of the unconvicted. And they offer nothing at all to the
unsentenced who now, as heretofore, are virtually indistinguishable
as far as the rules are concerned from sentenced prisoners. Our
study suggests that if few unconvicted prisoners were able to provide themselves with personal newspapers, books and other services
in 1971 then the majority of them are unlikely to benefit from the
new entitlements.

In chapter 4 we made much of the fact that it was intended that
remand centres should be governed by special rules and not by Prison
Rules. No special rules have emerged. Moreover, in practice, the
remand centres have done little more than duplicate the organisation
and regime of the local prison. We do not advocate, for reasons
given below, either the expansion or the retention of remand centres
as presently constituted and in consequence there would be little
point now in the belated development of special rules for remand
centres. Rather we take the view that new rules are required to
govern the lives of all unconvicted and unsentenced prisoners whatever their age or sex and wherever they may be held. If, as a
result of implementing such rules, a real distinction emerged
between the custody of those persons who have and those who have not
been sent to prison as a punishment then there would be no need for
remand centres as the specialist institutions which we now know and
which in our view have failed in their purpose. We are aware of the
fact that Prison Department has a legacy of buildings many of which
they would gladly consign to the bulldozer if they could. We are
also conscious of the fact that some of our proposals will be costly
and that we make them at a time when funds are likely to be limited.
However because of these very factors, and because Prison Department
has a large development programme in hand, we believe that it is all

the more necessary to take stock and to proclaim our objectives.
Only if we set clear standards will we be able to derive a measure
of the success or failure of our endeavours which goes beyond either
administrative convenience or the simple absorption, at the lowest
cost, of those persons whom the courts commit to custody. Some of
our proposals could be put into effect almost overnight. That
others would take much longer should not blind us to their desirability.

In our view the keynote of the rules for unconvicted prisoners
should be that such persons might suffer no greater loss of liberty
than that necessarily arising out of the fact of their confinement.
In order to achieve this it would be essential to reverse the
present policy whereby modest increments in the rights of the unconvicted, over and above those of the convicted and sentenced, have
to be justified by special provision in the Rules. Instead we
should insist that the unconvicted prisoner should enjoy the same
rights as the person remanded on bail, in so far as these may be
compatible with the requirement that he be kept in safe custody.
That is, that the onus should be placed on the Prison Department to
justify any decrements in the rights of the unconvicted, and that
these decrements should be the minimum consistent with the security
considerations at stake in each case. This perspective is derived
from the presumption that, until sentence is passed, custody is a
temporary device imposed not as a punishment but as a safeguard for
the due process of justice where there are reasonable grounds for
thinking either that the individual is unwilling to meet the requirements of the law or else that he constitutes a danger to the
public. Approximately one-half of all unconvicted prisoners subsequently receive a non-custodial sentence. There are thus good
grounds for viewing pre-trial detainees as a transitory group for
whom the emphasis in their management should be normalcy - continuity with that which preceded and will follow their custody. The
rules which we propose would stress that notion of humane containment which is introduced in the White Paper 'People in Prison' and
which we believe to be consistent with the objective outlined.

We are aware that while, for essentially legal reasons, the aims
which we have presented should be unchallengeable in the case of unconvicted prisoners, the position is more complex in the case of the
unsentenced. For these prisoners the presumption of innocence has
been shattered by conviction. And while it is true that half of
these also do not receive custodial sentences, it is clear that
prison staff are able to predict with a fair degree of certainty
that those convicted of the more serious crimes will be returned to
prison on sentence. However there are as many unsentenced prisoners
for whom no such safe predictions can be made, and yet, at present,
all unsentenced persons are dealt with by the authorities as though
for all practical purposes they were already sentenced to imprisonment. It seems to us worthwhile considering whether there may not
be ways of discriminating in the treatment of unsentenced prisoners
who fall into different categories. For example, just as the Criminal Justice Act 1967 prescribes that for persons accused of particular categories of offences the granting of bail is mandatory or discretionary, so it might be determined that unsentenced prisoners
convicted of certain offences should be subject to the same custodi-

al rules as unconvicted persons, while others convicted of more
serious offences should be subject to the same rules as sentenced
prisoners. We suggest that a working party be set up to consider
this issue in greater detail.

The provision of a regime for all unconvicted prisoners which
would be consistent with our views will of necessity be a longterm
aim. Some of our proposals could hardly be put into practice in the
present local prisons; others could be effected at the stroke of a
pen. In listing our proposals we recognise that from time to time
Prison Department might need to withhold facilities from some
prisoners in some circumstances. But the inability to use facilities should result from a justified deprivation rather than the
absence of facilities or their routine disregard. In our view the
regime for unconvicted prisoners should involve:

1   living accommodation which is physically separate from that
    provided for sentenced persons, though not necessarily in a
    different building;

2   the provision of day-rooms sufficient to permit prisoners to
    spend the greater proportion of their day outside their cells;

3   the provision of an educational and recreational programme in
    addition to work for those who wish to participate;

4   the provision of money for personal consumption at a level
    which should be no less than the current allowance awarded
    under supplementary benefits: we see no reason why unconvict-
    ed prisoners should not be entitled to claim supplementary,
    unemployment, or other benefits, if normally eligible to do
    so, whilst they are in prison;

5   the provision of radio, television and library facilities on
    a scale at least as generous as that available to sentenced
    prisoners;

6   every encouragement to retain personal clothing and effects
    including the provision of laundry facilities and, where
    eligible, ability to obtain a clothing grant from the De-
    partment of Health and Social Security for the purchase of
    suitable clothing;

7   a standard of cell furnishing and comfort commensurate with
    that available in modest but wholesome furnished accommodation
    outside, and including sufficient wardrobe and storage space;

8   facilities to receive visits in open conditions at all reason-
    able times, and without undue restriction on the length of
    visits during those periods, and to both send and receive
    letters and make telephone calls, under supervision if neces-
    sary, at the prisoner's expense.

Such a list is not exhaustive, and it is additional to such
rights as are already guaranteed to the unconvicted. It represents
in our view a reasonable expectation for persons who must be regard-

ed as innocent until proven guilty and many of whom will on sentence
not be considered to be in need of custodial treatment. Clearly
Prison Department must be given discretionary powers in each case.
Some prisoners, those charged jointly or those whose behaviour might
be dangerous to others, cannot be permitted to mix freely in day-
rooms (though that is not to say that they cannot mix at all). From
what we know of the unconvicted prison population the proportion of
persons in these categories is likely to be small. It may also be
necessary, in the interests of security, to ensure that prisoner
communication with the outside world is appropriately supervised.

As a first priority we have argued that accommodation for the unconvicted should be physically separate from that provided for
sentenced prisoners and we have suggested that the unsentenced might
be apportioned among those two categories on the basis of some
classification of their offence. But we should stress that we consider it equally important that unconvicted prisoners be kept in
close proximity to their local community. In consequence we do not
expect remand units in themselves to enjoy the supposed 'benefits of
scale' that come with large catchment areas. It will not always be
possible, therefore, to provide work or classes for unconvicted
persons alone. Where this is the case and where remand units are
part of a larger prison complex we consider that such activities
might be provided for more than one category of prisoner and that
unconvicted persons wishing to participate might, in order to do so,
sign away their right to be separated from sentenced persons.

Our proposals have implications for the staffing of remand units.
If continued contact with the community as well as safe custody are
to be the goals of remand units then it will be necessary to reconsider the job specification of the officers who staff them. At
present a prisoner's contact with the community is almost exclusive-
ly the concern of a small and over-stretched non-uniformed staff -
principally the prison welfare officers and to a lesser extent the
governor grades and other specialists. In spite of the continuing
deliberations of a long-standing Whitley Council joint working party
concerned with expanding the role of the modern prison officer, uni-
formed staff still spend their time primarily in maintaining the
internal good order of the prison and the safe custody of the
prisoners. With a few notable exceptions they are given scant encouragement, either through the example of their superiors or
through the constraints of their required duties, to become at all
concerned in the welfare or other problems of their charges. It
seems to us time to face up to the logic of the tasks involved and
to staff them accordingly, rather than to be bound, as first the
Mountbatten and then the Radzinowicz enquiries were bound, by considerations of esprit de corps in opposing any hard and fast distinction between different types of prison officers. Of course
anyone who works in a prison must be concerned to some extent with
security. But we do not think certain custodial tasks are compatible
with the aim of establishing staff-prisoner relationships which
could foster habilitative or rehabilitative processes between the
prisoner, his home and his community. There seems no more appropriate place to begin to change the relationship between security and
other duties than in those parts of institutions given over to the
detention of persons before trial or sentence.

We propose that prison officers in remand units should be divided

into two separate and specialist divisions. One would consist of
officers who would not be in uniform, who would be responsible for
the supervision of routine prisoner activities in the unit, and who
whose duty it would be to help prisoners maintain ties with the
community and resolve such problems as had resulted from their
custody. Such officers would be expected to have knowledge of, and
to work with, outside agencies and should be trained so to do.
Overall responsibility for at least some of their activities might
be vested in the prison welfare officer. Not all prison officers
would have either the desire or the capacity to engage in this type
of work. In any case it is desirable that some prison staff be spe-
cifically charged with a responsibility for security, and not be engaged in relationships or activities which could in any sense,
however remote, prejudice the carrying out of their duties. A
second group of officers would thus wear uniforms and would undertake perimeter patrols (including dog patrols where applicable),
gate duties, 'locks, bolts and bars' checks, cell and prisoner
searches, and when called upon, the removal of violent or disruptive
prisoners to separate accommodation. They too would require training, but of a kind that is now well established within the prison
service. How many staff should be allocated to each division would
be a matter for careful consideration, but it is worth pointing out
that such proposals are by no means inconsistent with the present
functional group working schemes recently introduced. Moreover, if
precedents are required, some such organisation appears to have been
implicit in the arrangements for internal order in our very first
penitentiary at Millbank one hundred and fifty years ago.

We have argued throughout this report that the optimism concerning the positive value of imprisonment which characterised 'Penal
Practice in a Changing Society' has rightly given way to the more
pessimistic, and in some respects more realistic, view which is reflected in 'People in Prison'. Linked to this change of view has
been the growing feeling that if prisons do no good then their potential harm should be mitigated by maintaining prisoners in reasonable proximity to the communities from whence they came and to which
they will return. In our view a policy of localised custody is of
importance for all prisoners, except perhaps those for whom security
considerations would rule it out, although given existing facilities
first priority should be given to trial and remand prisoners.
Prison Department appears generally to share this view at least in
principle. However, in the case of persons under 21 years the Department has decided that any need for localised custody should be
subordinated to the need to ensure that young prisoners do not
suffer the same privations as adults who are housed in old Victorian
buildings (Cmnd 5037, 1972, chapter 3). This is the raison d'être
of the remand centre building programme. But if the evidence we
have adduced from Winchester remand centre is typical then most
remand centres will have lost the advantage of locality for no obvious return in more humane standards of containment. The recent Advisory Council report on 'Young Adult Offenders', which puts considerable weight on the 'neighbourhood' custody principle, recog-
nises part of this argument. The report notes that until the number
of remand centres is substantially increased, where the choice of
location is between a convenient local prison and a more distant

remand centre then 'the balance of advantage may lie with the local prison' (Advisory Council, 1974, para.460) and they recommend that small remand centres should be constructed convenient to all the main centres of population (para.462). We disagree with the Advisory Council only in that we are not convinced that remand centres, as opposed to local prisons, will necessarily provide a regime more in keeping with the needs of either young or adult untried prisoners. The existing Prison Department establishments which are most convenient to centres of urban population are the local prisons and the three remand centres attached to local prisons. In our view these are the establishments around which our future penal policy should develop and, unless new urban remand units are opened, these are the prisons within which our unconvicted and unsentenced prisoners of all ages should be confined. Those persons at present housed in separate remand centres would generally derive some benefit in terms of convenience from transfer to these establishments and would probably suffer no great disadvantage in terms of the conditions of their custody. To the extent that disadvantages did ensue then our resources would be better spent in upgrading the conditions in the locals.

To argue the importance of local prisons is to argue for the redevelopment of our admittedly deficient existing institutions and for the acquisition of further urban sites. Both of these objectives would involve a building programme very different from that being completed and projected until 1978 (the details which follow are derived from the Annual Report of the Prison Department for 1972. Cmnd 5375, App.2 as modified by Parliamentary Answer, May 1973, 'Hansard' vol.855, cols 1441-5). The present building programme is the largest since the nineteenth century and it largely ignores the local prisons. If we exclude those new establishments which first opened prior to April 1972, the total published building programme at the time of writing involves an additional 19,095 places: of these, 589 places, or 3.08 per cent, are to be provided in local prisons - an additional 205 at Holloway, and 192 each at Bristol and Liverpool. A further 2,135 places, or 11.18 per cent, are to be provided in remand centres or remand centre/borstal allocation complexes and of these only 60, at Norwich, are on a local prison site. The remaining remand centre programme involves the expansion of the outlying centres at Pucklechurch, Low Newton and Thorp Arch and the building of new centres at Rochester, Glen Parva, North Weald and Feltham - all sites which suffer from similar or worse communication handicaps than those which characterise the existing centres and of which we have been so critical. In more than a decade only eight local prisons have figured at all prominently in the building programme - apart from minor refurbishing and security work - and even there the alterations do not amount to much. Holloway is the only local to be rebuilt and when that is complete it will have almost doubled its certified accommodation. Seven locals have recently had existing buildings converted or new units added to them or will do so in the near future: Winchester and Exeter have had remand centres attached to an existing site and Norwich is similarly to be expanded; Gloucester, Bristol and Liverpool have new wings either completed or in the process of building; Cardiff has had an existing wing converted into a remand centre.

Liverpool is the only local establishment still involved in the
programme for the financial year 1973-4. No local prison is included in the building programme for which planning clearance is held to
start during the period 1974-7, and no new urban location is included in the list of sites for which planning clearance is sought to
start in 1975-8.

The local prisons really feature in the building programme only
in a negative sense. Part of the rationale for constructing new,
and expanding existing, closed training prisons (predominantly category C but including a number of category B/A dispersal prisons) is
to reduce the overcrowding in the locals and to ensure that men
serving sentences of six months or more do so in a training prison.
But, as we argued in chapter 1, the most that could be expected from
such a building strategy would be the eventual elimination of overcrowding - assuming there were no further rises in population - and
the multi-functional nature of the local prisons would be left un-
touched. Despite some indications that Prison Department would like
to take the neighbourhood principle into account, the list of new
training prison sites, work on some of which is by now well advanced, includes locations which will rival Dartmoor, Portland and
the Isle of Wight for geographical inaccessibility. In the financial year 1972/3, for example, work was reported to be in
progress on three new category C prisons - Acklington in Northumber-
land, not far from Morpeth, Channings Wood in Devon, a few miles
from Newton Abbot, and Wrabness on the Suffolk coast near Manning-
tree. To these we may add the expansion, in the same year, of
Haverigg, near Millom in Cumberland, Northeye, near Bexhill in
Sussex, and the Verne, on Portland Bill in Dorset. The list could
be extended three-fold were we to name all the various training
prison sites projected to 1978. Sixty-one per cent of the published
building programme, providing 11,634 places, is devoted to the construction of training prisons which though regionalised are large,
rural and with few exceptions so isolated that visitors will require
the help of the Ordnance Survey to find them.

What is remarkable is that this huge programme has been introduced with so little debate and on the basis of little or no published
evidence as to the effectiveness of one or another type, size or
location of prison. It is worth noting, therefore, that in our comparative research into prison regimes we found rather fewer differences between the training prisons that we studied and what was
offered to convicted prisoners in the local prison at Winchester
than might have been expected (R.D.King, 1972). The differences
which favoured training prisons were not so much in the area of activities with a specific training or therapeutic content, but involved the provision of a reasonably full, and sometimes more interesting day's work with correspondingly more time out of cells.
There were also differences in some of the procedures adopted in the
everyday management of prisoners but these were by no means always
more relaxed than those we found at Winchester. Such differences
were important of course. But there seemed no obvious reason why
anything that had been provided in the training prisons should not
also be provided in local prisons, so long as the value of local
facilities was recognised and the resources allocated appropriately.

The White Paper 'People in Prison' emphasised that the main

virtue of the local prisons is that they are in the right places to
serve their trial and remand function. That is, they are near the
courts they serve, and can use specialist services and recruit staff
and so on from the local community. But what the White Paper failed
to note, is that these virtues are just as important in the long run
for sentenced prisoners who will also have to be received back into
the community eventually. The White Paper acknowledged that the
basis of the present prison system is still the local prison and announced the setting up of a study group to explore 'what would be
involved in the complete redevelopment of one of our Victorian
prisons' and to consider the 'design of a local prison' (Cmnd 4214,
1969, para.166). Five years later these deliberations have still to
be made public and Prison Department remains committed to a building
programme which, in a time of economic stringency seems likely to
consume whatever expenditure on buildings is permitted.

We would hope that the current decline in government expenditure
may signal a halt in the present building programme and a thorough
reappraisal of future policy. It would, of course, be extremely
costly to build new local prisons in urban centres where these are
presently lacking and to redevelop and rebuild our existing ones.
But it may well be that to do so would provide a better investment
for the prison system of the future. To determine that would require very much more research than has yet been undertaken in
prison. It is to be hoped that the role of the local prison might
be reviewed, together with the effectiveness of the other institutions within the prison system, against the background of the
available or possible alternatives outside that system altogether.
At the very least it is perhaps not too much to hope that at a time
of the greatest building activity for a hundred years, resources
will be found for one new urban local prison designed more con-
veniently for its many purposes.

To argue for new multi-functional local prisons is not, of
course, to deny the importance which should be attached to the development of non-custodial alternatives to pre-trial and pre-
sentence custody. But given our analysis in chapter 5 of this
report, while we hope that the numbers of persons received into
custody on remand will fall, we cannot be optimistic that any great
reduction in the overall use of custodial places will be achieved.
In any case whatever the future of the local prisons may be, no-one
who commits a person there, whether under sentence or on remand,
should do so without knowing just what the conditions are like.
Fox, writing of these conditions for the unconvicted in 1952,
pointed out that they 'have never excited public comment of a
general nature'. We think it is high time that they did.

Chapter 7

POSTSCRIPT

Since the completion of this study there have been a number of developments without reference to which this report would be incomplete.

When we were writing up our findings the latest statistics then available to us related to the year 1972. Since then, of course, further statistics have been published. Broadly speaking the trends we sketched out in chapter 2 have continued. By 1974 the proportion of persons appearing before magistrates' courts and who were remanded in custody had fallen still further to 15.1 per cent. But during 1974 there were 136,395 receptions of all categories of prisoners, males and females, into Prison Department establishments: this represented a modest increase of 3.4 per cent over the 1972 figures which followed a similarly modest decrease during 1973 (Cmnd 6152). But whereas the numbers of civil and sentenced prisoners received in 1973 and 1974 fell, the numbers of untried and unsentenced prisoners received continued to rise - and in the case of the untried the rise has been a steep one. If remands under Section 26 of the Magistrates' Courts Act 1952 are classified with untried prisoners - as we did in chapter 2 - then the reception of untried prisoners has increased by 13.6 per cent since 1972 and that of unsentenced prisoners by 1.1 per cent, while the receptions of civil and sentenced prisoners have fallen by 16.2 and 2.2 per cent respectively. As a result untried and unsentenced prisoners continued to account for a growing proportion of the total receptions to Prison Department establishments - from 43.1 per cent in 1960 to 51.9 per cent in 1972 and to 55.1 per cent in 1974. The same pattern emerges in terms of the average daily population: the 5,081 untried and unsentenced prisoners held on average throughout 1974 accounted for 13.8 per cent of the population, compared to 12.3 per cent in 1972 and 7.7 per cent in 1960.

There is little doubt that the most dramatic increases since 1972 have occurred in the numbers of young, and especially of very young, persons received into custody. Indeed even the numbers of males and females under the age of 17, and of females between 17 and 20 years who were received under sentence increased during this period while the numbers of sentenced persons in other age and sex categories declined.

But there were even bigger increases both absolutely and proportionately among young persons received before trial. Detailed
comparisons with the figures we gave in chapter 2 are not possible
because the 1974 statistics do not distinguish persons remanded
under Section 26 by age. In recent years, however, it has been the
practice to classify these cases with other unsentenced persons, and
if we make the comparison on this basis the receptions of untried
males under 17 years have nearly doubled since 1972, while the receptions for untried females in this age group have nearly tripled.
Receptions of untried males and females between the ages of 17 and
20 have risen by one fifth and two fifths respectively, while receptions of men over 21 years rose by less than a tenth and the receptions of adult women fell by nearly a quarter. Of course, adults
still predominate among the receptions of untried persons: but of
the 6,321 extra receptions before trial in 1974 compared to 1972,
more than a quarter were accounted for by persons under 17 and
nearly half by persons between 17 and 20 years.

The trends for unsentenced prisoners closely resembled those for
sentenced prisoners when considered in terms of age. Thus receptions of males and females under the age of 17 increased by 29.3
and 53 per cent respectively, and the receptions of females between
17 and 20 years increased by 7.8 per cent, while the numbers of receptions in the remaining age and sex categories fell.

Taken together the numbers of trial and remand prisoners in the
average daily population of Prison Department establishments were
higher in 1974 than at any time in the period considered in this
monograph. We understand from the Home Office that the figures for
1975 will reveal a continuation of these trends, with the pressure
on secure accommodation especially in the remand centres reaching a
new high point during that summer. Not surprisingly Prison Department has been hard put to alleviate the conditions in local
prisons and remand centres, and we know of no developments that can
substantially have improved the circumstances of prisoners held
before trial and sentence and which we have described in this
volume. The growth in numbers of receptions in the youngest age
categories has meant that Prison Department has had to transfer some
of the 17-20 age group into the local prisons to make room for the
under 17s in the remand centres (Cmnd 6148, para.85). Even so considerable overcrowding in particular remand centres has occurred and
from time to time the Home Office has been forced to revise the
catchment areas of some centres accordingly. Winchester, like most
remand centres which are not on the edge of a major connurbation,
has had its catchment area greatly enlarged. It is now even more
likely that young untried and unsentenced prisoners will be held in
an establishment at some distance from their homes.

The ever-growing numbers of trial and remand prisoners have
stimulated further attempts to increase the proportion of defendants
awarded bail. In March 1975 the Secretary of State indicated that a
bill would be introduced to give statutory effect to some of the
recommendations of the Working Party on Bail Procedures in Magistrates' Courts (Home Office, 1974). The bill would probably include: a presumption in favour of bail; the extension of the
limited requirement under Section 18 (8) of the Criminal Justice Act
1967 to give reasons for refusing bail so that it applied to all

cases where bail is refused; the creation of an offence of absconding while on bail; and certain changes in the surety system
(Hansard, vol.888, col.533). In December 1975 the Secretary of
State said, in a written answer, that the Bail Bill would be introduced 'as soon as possible' (Hansard, vol.902, col.294).

Meanwhile on 8 October 1975 the Home Office issued a circular to
courts and chief officers of police, urging the introduction of
measures which might 'in some cases enable courts to grant bail
where they might otherwise have remanded in custody' or which might
'enable the period of time spent in custody on remand to be reduced'
(Home Office Circular No.155/1975, Bail Procedures). Among the
practices commended are: the use of bail questionnaires in order to
increase the level of information available to the court concerning
the defendant's community ties (developed by the Camberwell Green
Bail Project conducted by the Vera Institute of Criminal Justice in
collaboration with the Inner London Probation Service); the greater
use of bail conditions such as reporting to the police; the use of
bail hostels (more than a dozen bail or approved probation hostels
are now available); the use of prison out-patient facilities for
the preparation of medical reports; and the restriction of remands
in custody pending completion of police enquiries to the minimum
necessary period.

We greatly welcome these developments, although how much impact
they will have on the numbers of persons remanded in custody remains
to be seen. The direct attack on improving the conditions for
persons who are remanded in custody is still to begin.

RDK

RM

January 1976

BIBLIOGRAPHICAL INDEX

ADVISORY COUNCIL (1968), 'The Regime for Long-term Prisoners in Conditions of Maximum Security', Report of the Advisory Council on the Penal System (Radzinowicz Report), HMSO. (5,90)

ADVISORY COUNCIL (1974), 'Young Adult Offenders', Report of the Advisory Council on the Penal System (Younger Report), HMSO. (3,8, 91,92)

BANKS, C. (1968), Prison Receptions and Population, paper read at Third National Conference on Research and Teaching in Criminology, Cambridge, July. (14)

BLOM-COOPER, L. (1973), Bail Hostels, 'Justice of the Peace', 17 March, vol.137, p.167. (3)

BOTTOMLEY, A.K. (1970), 'Prison Before Trial', Occasional Papers in Social Administration, no.39, Bell. (3,68,72)

BOTTOMLEY, A.K. (1974), 'Decisions in the Penal Process', Martin Robertson. (3)

DAVIES, C. (1970), Why Risley Should be Closed, 'New Society', 8 January. (4,47,48,68)

DAVIES, C. (1971), Pre-trial Imprisonment: a Liverpool Study, 'Brit. Journal Criminol', vol.II, January. (3)

ELKIN, W.A. (1957), 'The English Penal System', Penguin. (32)

FOUCAULT, M. (1967), 'Madness and Civilisation', Tavistock. (4)

FOX, Sir Lionel (1952), 'The English Prison and Borstal System', Routledge & Kegan Paul. (2,4,32,33,40,50,63,94)

HALL WILLIAMS, J.E. (1965), The Use the Courts Make of Prison, 'Soc.Rev.Monogr.', no.9, University of Keele. (6)

HMSO (1967), 'Royal Commission on the Penal System: Written Evidence from Government Departments, Miscellaneous Bodies and Individual Witnesses'. (50)

HOME OFFICE (1974), 'Bail Procedures in Magistrates' Courts', Report of the Working Party, HMSO. (2,3,96)

HOME OFFICE PRISON DEPARTMENT (Various Dates), Standing Orders and Circular Instructions. (36,37,51,63,64,84,85,86,87,97)

HORU (1960), 'Time Spent Awaiting Trial', Home Office Research Unit Report no.2, HMSO. (2,3,68,72)

HORU (1974), 'The Use of Bail and Custody by London Magistrates' Courts Before and After the C.J.A. 1967', Home Office Research Unit Report no.20, HMSO. (3)

KING, M. (1971), 'Bail or Custody?', Cobden Trust. (3,4,39,68)
KING, R.D. (1972), An Analysis of Prison Regimes, unpublished
interim report on the work of the Prison Regimes Project, University
of Southampton. (40,93)
KING, R.D. RAYNES, N.V. and TIZARD, J. (1971), 'Patterns of Resi-
dential Care: Sociological Studies in Institutions for Handicapped
Children', Routledge & Kegan Paul. (40)
KLARE, H.J. (1964), The Problem of Remand in Custody for Diagnostic
Purposes, in Lopez-Rey and Germain (eds), 'Studies in Penology to
the Memory of Sir Lionel Fox', Martinus Nijhoff. (6)
NIE, N. BENT, D.H. and HULL, C.H. (1970), 'Statistical Package for
the Social Sciences', McGraw-Hill. (44)
ROTHMAN, D.J. (1971), 'The Discovery of the Asylum', Little, Brown.
(4)
SHEFFÉ, M. (1943), On Solutions of the Behrens-Fisher Problem Based
on the T-distribution, 'Ann.Math.Stats.', 14, 35. (44)
SPARKS, R.F. (1971), 'Local Prisons: The Crisis in the English Penal
System', Heinemann. (4,5,14,24,29)
ZANDER, M. (1967), Bail: a Reappraisal, 'Criminal Law Review', 25.
(3)
ZANDER, M. (1971), A Study of Bail/Custody Decisions in London
Magistrates' Courts, 'Criminal Law Review', p.191, April. (3,39)

Command papers

Cmnd 645 (1959), White Paper, 'Penal Practice in a Changing So-
ciety', HMSO. (6,7,10,17,91)
Cmnd 1289 (1961), 'Report of the Interdepartmental Committee on the
Business of the Criminal Courts'(Streatfeild Report), HMSO. (63)
Cmnd 1467 (1961), 'Report of the Commissioners of Prisons for the
Year 1960', HMSO. (19,21)
Cmnd 2030 (1963), 'Report of the Commissioners of Prisons for the
Year 1962', HMSO. (10)
Cmnd 3088 (1966), 'Report on the Work of the Prison Department
1965', HMSO. (19)
Cmnd 3175 (1966), Report of the Inquiry into Prison Escapes and
Security (Mountbatten Report), HMSO. (5,11,90)
Cmnd 3408 (1967), 'Report on the Work of the Prison Department
1966', HMSO. (7)
Cmnd 4186 (1969), 'Report on the Work of the Prison Department
1968', HMSO. (7,21)
Cmnd 4214 (1969), White Paper, 'People in Prison', HMSO. (5,7,14,
24,47,49,50,60,88,91,93,94)
Cmnd 4266 (1969), 'Report on the Work of the Prison Department
1968, Statistical Tables', HMSO. (21)
Cmnd 4724 (1971), 'Report on the Work of the Prison Department
1970', HMSO. (6,10,17)
Cmnd 4829 (1971), White Paper 'Public Expenditure to 1975-76', HMSO.
(14)
Cmnd 5037 (1972), 'Report on the Work of the Prison Department
1971', HMSO. (7,8,17,91)
Cmnd 5156 (1972), 'Report on the Work of the Prison Department
1971, Statistical Tables', HMSO. (70,72)

Cmnd 5178 (1972), White Paper, 'Public Expenditure to 1976-77',
HMSO. (14)
Cmnd 5375 (1973), 'Report on the Work of the Prison Department
1972', HMSO. (7,8,21,49,53,68,92)
Cmnd 4502 (1973), 'Criminal Statistics, England and Wales 1972',
HMSO. (65,66)
Cmnd 5489 (1973), 'Report on the Work of the Prison Department
1972, Statistical Tables', HMSO. (1,20,21,24,66)
Cmnd 5519 (1973), White Paper, 'Public Expenditure to 1977-78',
HMSO. (14)
Cmnd 6148 (1975), 'Report on the Work of the Prison Department
1974', HMSO. (96)
Cmnd 6152 (1975), 'Report on the Work of the Prison Department
1974, Statistical Tables', HMSO. (95)

Statutes

1865 c.126   Prisons Act 1865. (50)
1877 c.21   Prisons Act 1877. (31,33)
1898 c.41   Prisons Act 1898. (50)
1933 c.46   Children and Young Persons Act 1933. (17)
1948 c.58   Criminal Justice Act 1948. (17,19,27,47,48,49,50)
1952 c.52   Prisons Act 1952. (30,49,50)
1952 c.55   Magistrates' Courts Act 1952. (15,17,26,27,30,63,64,
             66,67,69,75,76,95)
1959 c.72   Mental Health Act 1959. (69,82)
1961 c.39   Criminal Justice Act 1961. (63)
1967 c.80   Criminal Justice Act 1967. (16,24,26,66,88,96)
1969 c.54   Children and Young Persons Act 1969. (17,27)
1971 c.23   Courts Act 1971. (68)
1972 c.71   Criminal Justice Act 1972. (3)

Statutory instruments

1952 no.1432   Detention Centre Rules 1952. (51)
1958 no.1990   Attendance Centre Rules 1958. (51)
1964 no.387   Borstal Rules 1964. (51)
1964 no.388   Prison Rules 1964. (30,31,32,34,36,37,39,40,57,58,
               59,60,62,84,85,87,88)
1968 no.440   Prison (Amendment) Rules 1968. (30)